The
Grammar
Devotional

Also by Mignon Fogarty

*Grammar Girl's Quick and Dirty Tips
for Better Writing*

The
Grammar
Devotional

DAILY TIPS for SUCCESSFUL WRITING from GRAMMAR GIRL™

MIGNON FOGARTY

St. Martin's Griffin
New York

"A rule is just a style with an army."
—ANDREW SCHWALM

(A play on the more well-known quotation from an unknown student of the Yiddish linguist Max Weinreich: "A language is just a dialect with an army and navy.")

www.stmartins.com

Design by Meryl Sussman Levavi
Illustrations by Arnie Ten

The Library of Congress has cataloged the Henry Holt edition as follows:

Fogarty, Mignon.
    The grammar devotional : daily tips for successful writing from grammar girl / Mignon Fogarty. — 1st Holt paperbacks ed.
        p. cm.
    "A Holt Paperback."
    Includes bibliographical references and index.
    ISBN 978-0-8050-9165-6
    1. English language—Grammar. 2. English language—Rhetoric. 3. Report writing. I. Title.
    PE1112.F6125 2009
    428.2—dc22   2009023847

ISBN 978-0-8050-9165-6

Originally published in hardcover format by Henry Holt and Company

10 9 8 7 6 5 4 3 2

The
Grammar
Devotional

Introduction

People are often moved and challenged by nuggets gleaned on a daily basis—whether from a spiritual devotional, a tip-a-day calendar, or a regularly e-mailed newsletter. But there are few groups who need constant encouragement more than writers—it is, after all, a mostly solitary practice. *The Grammar Devotional*, then, is here to help you: it has daily reminders of our basic tenets (*who* versus *whom*, anyone?); inspiring profiles of writers and grammarians who have helped English evolve to what it is today; and quizzes, word scrambles, and word searches to help solidify newly learned tips.

English is a messy language. Unlike French, we don't have a council to decide how we should write or speak. We only have a multitude of competing college handbooks, dictionaries, and usage and style guides, such as *The Chicago Manual of Style* and *The Associated Press Stylebook*, which frequently disagree. Space is tight in this book, and I like to keep things simple, but wherever possible I point out when something is a style rather than a rule. Too many people go around believing the way they learned to do things is the only way to do things, when really it's just one of the acceptable choices.

As you will see, the book is organized by generic weeks so you can start any time. It's meant to be read through, just like a devotional, but we've also included an index so you can use the book as a reference guide and quickly find specific tips when you need them. Most of the time, punctuation is on Monday, Language Rock Stars are on Wednesday, quizzes and word scrambles are on Friday, and word search puzzles and cartoons are on Sunday, although I occasionally deviate from this pattern to keep related entries together.

It may seem like a trivial endeavor, a tip each day, but at the end of a year the knowledge adds up. A year's worth of new knowledge can imbue your writing with new confidence. Here's to better e-mail messages, essays, marketing materials, articles, and novels.

THE BURGER OF MCDONALD'S: MAKING POSSESSIVE NAMES POSSESSIVE

Have you ever wondered how to make a possessive name such as *McDonald's*, *Carl's*, or *St. Anthony's* possessive?

The short answer is don't! Rewrite the sentence to avoid such a construction because, technically, you're supposed to add another apostrophe or apostrophe and *s* on the end—which looks ridiculous.

> **McDonald's's earnings were super-sized last quarter. (technically correct)**

> **McDonald's' earnings were super-sized last quarter. (technically correct)**

> **McDonald's reported super-sized earnings last quarter. (better)**

See page 75 to learn why there are two competing technically correct answers.

I LOVE YOU: SUBJECT VERSUS OBJECT

To figure out things such as when to use *who* or *whom* or *lay* or *lie*, you need to be able to identify the subject and object of a sentence.

Fortunately, it's easy! The subject is the person or thing doing something, and the object is having something done to it.

Just remember the sentence *I love you. I* is the subject. *You* is the object of the sentence and also the object of my affection. How's that? You are the object of my affection and the object of my sentence. It's like a Valentine's Day card and grammar trick all rolled into one.

Language Rock Star: Jed Hartman and the Law of Prescriptivist Retaliation

Hartman's Law of Prescriptivist Retaliation, coined by technical writer Jed Hartman in his Web-based column, Words & Stuff (http://www.kith.org/logos/words/words.html), states that "any article or statement about correct grammar, punctuation, or spelling is bound to contain at least one eror." It is sometimes also known as McKean's Law after lexicographer Erin McKean or Skitt's Law for alt.usage.english (http://www .alt-usage-english.org) contributor Skitt, both of whom appear to have independently made the same observation. Any errors you find in this text were put there intentionally as a test to see if you are paying attention. Honest.

So Many Talents: Not Only . . . But Also

When *not only* is followed by *but also* (or simply *but*), it's considered good form to make sure the parts that follow each set of words are formatted the same way.

> **He is not only <u>a great swimmer</u>, but also <u>a great musician</u>. (Good: the sentence uses two noun clauses, which are underlined.)**

> **He is not only <u>a great swimmer</u>, but also <u>plays amazing music</u>. (Bad: the sentence uses a noun clause and a verb clause. It's bad because they don't match.)**

You could make the second example better by rewriting it with two verb clauses:

> **He not only <u>swims with ease</u>, but also <u>plays amazing music</u>.**

Quiz: You're Welcome

Which of the following is incorrect?

    a. Squiggly received a warm welcome.
    b. Please welcome Squiggly.
    c. Squiggly's arrival was a welcome distraction.
    d. You're welcomed.
    e. They welcomed Squiggly to the family.
    f. Welcome!

The answer and an explanation are on page 211.

A Supposed Rule:
Supposedly Versus *Supposably*

It would be much easier if I could tell you that *supposably* isn't a word, but I can't. It is a word, but the problem is that *supposably* doesn't mean the same thing as *supposedly* and most people use it incorrectly.

The word you usually want is *suppos<u>ed</u>ly*, which means roughly "assumed to be true" and almost always includes a hint of sarcasm or disbelief:

Supposedly, he canceled our date because of a family emergency.

She supposedly sent the check, but it was lost in the mail.

Supposably means "supposable," "conceivable," or "arguably." It is only a valid word in American English; the British wisely refuse to accept it.

THAT PROBLEM

Always make sure your *thats* are necessary. For example, these two sentences mean the same thing, so you can leave out the *that*.

The sandwich that I ate yesterday was delicious.

The sandwich   I ate yesterday was delicious.

If your sentence has multiple *thats*, see if you can take some out without changing the meaning.

I know that she would prefer that people call her Cookie.

I know   she would prefer that people call her Cookie.

Unfortunately, many people delete *thats* even when they're needed for clarity. Here's an example of a sentence that could initially confuse readers when you omit the word *that*:

Aardvark maintains Squiggly's yard is too large. (wrong)

Because there's no *that* after *maintains*, readers could initially believe that Aardvark takes care of (maintains) Squiggly's lawn until they reach the phrase *is too large*. A *that* makes it clear Aardvark has an opinion, not a job.

Aardvark maintains that Squiggly's yard is too large.

Aardvark maintains Squiggly's yard.

Aardvark maintains that Squiggly's yard is too large.

And per se And: Ampersands

The ampersand (&) is a symbol for *and*. Unlike the percent or degree symbol, you generally shouldn't use the ampersand except in the most informal situations. Some style guides allow them as part of a formal company name (Smith & Wesson, Tiffany & Co.). Other style guides recommend spelling out the *and* in such cases. Most style guides recommend using the ampersand when the rest of the name is also an abbreviation (AT&T) and in common expressions (R&D). As you see here, there are no spaces on either side of the ampersand when it is used in that way.

In common phrases, *and* can also be abbreviated using apostrophes for the missing letters: rock 'n' roll.

Shibboleth

People can be as passionate about language as they are about religion, and sometimes the two intersect. For example, linguists sometimes describe a word as a *shibboleth*. It means that the word tags you as a member of a certain group or class. For example, if you say *irregardless*, it tags you as someone who is poorly educated or doesn't use proper language.

Shibboleth is a Hebrew word, and its linguistic meaning stems from the Biblical story of the Gileadites, who used the word to identify Ephraimites. The Ephraimites could not pronounce the "sh" sound, so *shibboleth* came out sounding wrong, making them instantly identifiable.

LANGUAGE ROCK STAR: SAMUEL JOHNSON

Samuel Johnson was the lone author of *A Dictionary of the English Language*, which was arguably the most influential English dictionary from its publication in 1755 until the publication of the *Oxford English Dictionary* in 1928. It took Johnson nine years to write the nearly forty-three thousand entries. Although Johnson's dictionary was the first attempt at a comprehensive English dictionary and embraced the inclusion of multiple definitions and the use of illustrative quotations in a way no previous dictionary had, it also had biases and humor. For example, the definition for "lexicographer" included "a writer of dictionaries; a harmless drudge."

WHO? WHAT? WHICH? INTERROGATIVE PRONOUNS

It may seem odd that question words are pronouns. Don't pronouns stand in for nouns? Well, not all of them. The interrogative pronouns (*who, whom, what, which, whose, whoever, whomever, whatever, whichever*) are used to ask questions. Usually you can rewrite the answer to the question as the question itself with a noun or adjective in place of the pronoun.

Who wants chocolate? **Squiggly** wants chocolate.

Whom should we invite? We should invite **Aardvark**.

What is that class called? That class is called **Fondue Basics**.

Which car did they take? They took the **green** car.

Word Scramble: Types of Pronouns

There are six major types of pronouns. See if you can unscramble their names.

espalron_____

ssiseposve_____

dnsetmoivatre_____

ndiitnefei_____

riaetvel_____

tgteivoirrnae_____

The answer key is on page 211.

How Many Blondes Does It Take? *Blond* Versus *Blonde*

It sounds like a joke, but it's actually a legitimate question: How do you spell *blond*?

The word comes to English from French, in which it has masculine and feminine forms. As an English noun, it kept those two forms; thus, a blond is a fair-haired man and a blonde is a fair-haired woman. When you're using the word as an adjective, there is only one spelling: *blond*.

The blonde was delighted when Squiggly presented her with a dictionary.

She wondered whether Squiggly could be considered a blond. He was yellow, after all.

She had yellow-blond hair, but Squiggly only had yellow skin.

9

MYRIAD

I like myriad 10,000 Maniacs songs—"These Are Days," "Candy Everybody Wants," "Few and Far Between," and probably more that I can't think of right now. But do a few make a myriad?

The word *myriad* is derived from the Greek word for ten thousand and has long since come to mean "a whole bunch" or "an uncountable multitude," so it's hard to argue that *myriad* is a good way to describe three or four songs. *Various*, *a few*, or *many* would probably be better choices.

Another hot debate is whether it is correct to say, "The forest contains myriad species" or "The forest contains *a* myriad of species." You commonly hear "a myriad of" and just as commonly hear people railing that it should be simply "myriad" because the word is an adjective and essentially equivalent to a number. You wouldn't say "There are *a* ten thousand of species," so you shouldn't say "There are *a* myriad of species," so the argument goes.

Believe it or not, most language experts say that either way is fine. *Myriad* was actually used as a noun in English long before it was used as an adjective, and today it's considered both a noun and an adjective, which means it can be used with an *a* before it (as a noun) or without an *a* before it (as an adjective). Nevertheless, if you choose to say or write "a myriad of," I must warn you that you'll encounter occasional but vehement resistance. You may want to cut out this entry, laminate it, and carry it in your wallet as a defense.

SALUTATION SOLUTIONS: *HI* VERSUS *DEAR*

Technically, those e-mail messages you write should begin *Hi, John*—with a comma after *Hi*.

You see, *Hi, John* is different from *Dear John* because *hi* and *dear* are not the same kind of word. *Hi* is an interjection just like *wow* and *ugh*, and *dear* is an adjective that modifies John.

In *Hi, John* you are directly addressing John, which means the punctuation rules of direct address apply. From a comma-rules standpoint, *Hi, John* is no different from *Thanks for coming, John* or *Wow, John, what were you thinking?* You can end *Hi, John* with a period or, if you continue the sentence, a comma.

A BOOK FOR EVERYMAN: *EACH* AND *EVERY*

Each and *every* mean the same thing and are considered singular nouns so they take singular verbs. (Note the singular verbs in the following example.) If you want to get technical, you can use *each* to emphasize the individual items or people:

Each car is handled with care.

Inspectors scrutinize each egg to make sure it isn't cracked.

And you can use *every* to emphasize the larger group:

Every car should use hybrid technology.

The Egg Farmers of America want eggs on every table for breakfast.

People often say "each and every" for emphasis, but it is redundant, and I almost always advise brevity when it comes to usage.

Eager Beaver: *Anxious* Versus *Eager*

To some, *anxious* has more of a negative connotation than *eager*. You're eager for your long-distance boyfriend's plane to arrive, unless you're going to break up with him. Then you're more likely to be anxious for his plane to arrive so you can get it over with. *Anxious* is evolving, though. The distinction between the two terms was much stronger in the seventeenth century. Today, many people use the words interchangeably.

I'm eager to see the dessert tray. (standard)

I'm anxious to see my ex-wife. (standard)

I'm anxious to get our new puppy. (fine, but sometimes disputed)

Manners Beats Grammar: Ordering Pronouns

"Me first" is a bad attitude in life, and so it is in grammar, too. When you put yourself in a list with others, it's a rule of politeness to put yourself last:

Squiggly and I are shopping.

Please send the recipe to Squiggly, Aardvark, and me.

When you're combining nouns and pronouns, the rule is to put the pronouns first, unless that pronoun is *I* or *me*. (Politeness trumps the other rule.) Although the sentences below illustrate the rule, they sound awkward. In most cases, you'd probably use plural pronouns such as *they* and *us*.

She and Squiggly went shopping.

Please send the recipe to her and me.

Quiz: *Disc* Versus *Disk*

Circle the correct sentences below.

> **a. I stored my data on a compact disc.**
> **b. I have a slipped disc in my back.**
> **c. Does anyone use floppy disks anymore?**
> **d. The disk failed in my external hard drive.**

The answer and an explanation are on page 211.

An Important Distinction: *Historic* Versus *Historical*

Historical refers to anything from the past, important or not. For example, any past presidential inauguration would be a historical event, and any book that focuses on history or past events would be a historical book.

> **Grandpa collects historical inauguration photographs.**

> **Sir Fragalot enjoys historical novels.**

Historic refers to something important or influential in history.

> **Obama's inauguration was a historic event.**

> **The Gutenberg Bible is a historic book.**

You can remember the different meanings of *historic* and *historical* by thinking that the ending "ic" means important, and they both start with *i*, and "al" is "all in the past," and those both start with *a*.

CamelCase

CamelCase (also known as medial capitals, intercaps, hump-backing, CapWords, and BiCapitalials, among other names) is the practice that has now become trendy of promoting a letter in the middle of a word to uppercase. Most often the capital letter in the middle seems to result from squishing two words together that would normally be separated by a space (e.g., MySpace), but occasionally the capital just seems to pop up at a convenient syllable (e.g., OutKast).

Although the phenomenon can be traced back to at least the 1950s, it gained steam among computer programmers (probably because spaces are often discouraged or disallowed in programming, so a convenient way to highlight multiple words in a file name or variable is to capitalize the first letter of each squished-together word). More recently, marketers decided it was a trendy way to make a company name stand out.

If a formal company name uses CamelCase (e.g., YouTube, PayPal, TiVo), use that form in your writing. But other than honoring official names, leave the camel at the zoo—don't go around calling a plain old help desk a HelpDesk. It's definitely unnecessary!

Leave the camel at the zoo.

Parentheses and Punctuation

When a parenthetical statement falls at the end of a sentence, the placement of the terminal punctuation depends on whether the words inside the parentheses are a complete sentence.

If the words inside the parentheses *aren't* a complete sentence, the period, question mark, or exclamation point that ends the sentence goes after the parenthesis:

Squiggly likes chocolate (and nuts).

Could Aardvark bring home candy (quickly)?

If the words inside the parentheses *are* a complete sentence, the period, question mark, or exclamation point that ends the sentence goes inside the parenthesis:

Bring chocolate. (Squiggly likes sweets.)

Buy chocolate. (Bring it quickly!)

Sometimes I Hate Grammar: *Sometimes* Versus *Sometime* Versus *Some Time*

Want to hate English while feeling dark and moody? Note that these mean different things: *sometime, some time,* and *sometimes.* As I'm writing this tip I have the Depeche Mode song "Sometimes" in my head. *Sometimes* means "now and then" or "occasionally," so when they wrote the lyrics "Sometimes I question everything," they used it properly. Thank goodness! I'd hate my college memories to be tainted by a love of bad usage. *Sometime* means "at some unspecified time" and *some time* means "quite a while." *I'll dig out that old Depeche Mode tape sometime and spend some time listening to it again.*

Language Rock Star: Noah Webster

Noah Webster, of *Webster's Dictionary* fame, believed it was important for America, a new and revolutionary nation, to assert its cultural independence from Britain through language. He wrote the first American spelling, grammar, and reading schoolbooks and the first American dictionary. He was an advocate of spelling reform and is responsible for many of the differences between American and British English; for example, he introduced spellings such as *color* (versus *colour*) and *program* (versus *programme*). Merriam-Webster eventually acquired the rights to Webster's works and publishes the true descendants of the original Webster's dictionaries, but the term "Webster's" has entered the public domain and now also appears in titles of unrelated dictionaries.

The Him-lich Maneuver: *Who* Versus *Whom*

Do you choke when you have to decide when to use *who* and *whom*? Here's something I call the "him-lich maneuver." Ask if you could hypothetically answer the question with *him*. If you can, use *whom*. *Him* and *whom* both end with the letter *m*. This works because *whom* refers to objects, and *him* is an object pronoun, so it makes a good test case.

> **Who/Whom should we invite? (You could answer, "We should invite <u>him</u>." You've got a *him*, so the right choice is *whom*.)**

> **Who/Whom is going? (You could answer, "<u>He</u> is going." *Him* doesn't work, so the right choice is *who*.)**

Quiz: *Former* Versus *Latter*

In which sentence does Squiggly want chocolate?

a. Aardvark found canned tuna and chocolates in the cupboard. Squiggly craved the former.
b. Aardvark found canned tuna and chocolates in the cupboard. Squiggly craved the latter.

The answer and an explanation are on page 211.

You're Entitled to Your Opinion: *Titled* Versus *Entitled*

Some people think *entitled* shouldn't be used in this sense: *She sold her story, which was entitled "Squiggly and Aardvark Rule the World."* They are entitled to their opinion, but they are wrong. Of course, *entitled* can also indicate that someone has a certain right, but major dictionaries and usage guides state that *titled* and *entitled* are synonyms in the "name of a book, article, or speech" sense. Simpler is almost always better, though, and since *titled* is simpler than *entitled*, it's often the better choice. Better yet, rewrite the sentence without either word; it usually results in a simpler, more direct sentence: *She sold her story, "Squiggly and Aardvark Rule the World."*

WORD SEARCH: PREPOSITION ME!

Prepositions are words, such as *on, in, at,* and *by,* that describe relationships between other words—relationships such as position and time. These are some of the most difficult words for people learning English to understand; often, there's no reason why we use one preposition in a common phrase instead of another. Find some of the longer prepositions in the puzzle below.

The answer key is on page 212.

W	I	T	H	O	U	T	A	B	O	V	E	U
S	E	V	N	B	T	D	A	M	S	L	P	G
E	I	U	O	T	E	G	N	S	N	O	R	F
D	C	N	Q	O	A	F	O	O	N	E	F	T
I	D	N	S	I	E	R	O	E	Y	O	A	H
S	X	U	N	I	C	D	E	R	Z	E	T	R
E	W	S	R	A	D	W	I	T	E	C	B	O
B	T	I	B	I	T	E	I	S	Q	I	N	U
T	C	L	T	E	N	L	H	A	T	R	A	G
G	Q	F	B	H	L	G	N	G	B	U	R	H
T	U	O	H	G	U	O	R	H	T	O	O	E
D	O	R	T	N	D	R	A	W	O	T	U	I
U	Q	I	A	J	O	U	T	B	U	C	N	T
E	X	C	E	P	T	M	E	N	G	E	D	M
R	E	D	N	U	X	L	T	A	F	T	E	R
C	A	A	E	S	O	I	B	E	S	I	D	E
R	J	J	B	W	L	K	B	E	H	I	N	D

ABOUT	BEHIND	DURING	OUTSIDE	UPON
ABOVE	BELOW	EXCEPT	THROUGH	WITH
ACROSS	BENEATH	FOR	THROUGHOUT	WITHOUT
AFTER	BESIDE	INSIDE	TILL	
AGAINST	BESIDES	NEAR	TOWARD	
AROUND	BETWEEN	OFF	UNDER	
BEFORE	BEYOND	OUT	UNTIL	

It's a Bird. It's a Plane. It's Super Period!
Abbreviated Endings

When you end a sentence with an abbreviation, you don't need an extra period.

Apple Computer, Inc. became Apple, Inc.. (wrong)

The period that ends the abbreviation also ends the sentence. Think of it as an environmentally friendly rule—one dot of ink serves two purposes.

However, such sentences can confuse readers because it may not be obvious that you've started a new sentence. Try to rewrite the sentence so the abbreviation doesn't come at the end or write out the abbreviated word.

The story is different when the sentence is a question or exclamation—then you need both punctuation marks:

Why did they choose Apple, Inc.?

I adore their name—Apple, Inc.!

Where's That Line Again? *Standing On Line*

Listeners often ask me about the regionalism in which people say *on line* instead of *in line* to mean they are physically waiting in a row with other people. There's nothing grammatically incorrect about using *on line* to mean standing in line; it just sounds strange to people who aren't used to hearing it, which is generally anyone who doesn't live in New York City, New Jersey, Connecticut, Massachusetts, or parts of Philadelphia. A Google search I've been conducting for the last few years suggests that *standing on line* is gaining popularity relative to *standing in line*, but it's still about four and a half times less common.

Sing it Loudly: Between You and Me

When a song with a grammatically incorrect title becomes a smash hit, that's a catastrophe. English teachers everywhere were surely gnashing their teeth as students sang along with "Between You and I" by Jessica Simpson in 2006. But she can be forgiven; it's a hypercorrection heard sputtering from the mouths of many educated people. The reason it's wrong is that *between* is a preposition, and it's a rule that pronouns following prepositions have to be in the objective case. *Me* is the objective pronoun; *I* is a subjective pronoun. Don't worry about the details, just clear your mind of the song and memorize that the correct phrase is *between you and me*.

Accident Prone: *On Accident* Versus *By Accident*

Nobody knows why, but young people all over the United States have started saying *on accident* instead of *by accident*. A fascinating linguistic study by Leslie Barratt showed that *on accident* followed an age distribution: If you're under twelve, you probably say *on accident*. If you're over thirty-seven, you probably say *by accident*. People between those ages show mixed use: some say *on accident* and some say *by accident*. There's a theory (that I don't buy) that says children are seeking parallelism with *on purpose*. Have you ever known kids to seek parallelism? There isn't much of a stigma associated with saying *on accident*, so as those kids grow up it's likely to become the standard phrase.

Quiz: Can Not Versus Cannot

Which spelling is more common?

a. I cannot see the carrot?
b. I can not see the carrot?

The answer and an explanation are on page 212.

I'm One Up on You: One Versus You

A school of thought (to which I don't subscribe) believes it is wrong to write a sentence that uses *you* in the following way:

It's the kind of cold that makes <u>you</u> too tired to even watch TV.

They believe it should be written using the word *one*:

It's the kind of cold that makes <u>one</u> too tired to even watch TV.

It's not wrong to write the sentence using *one*, but it does make one sound formal and stuffy. One is likely to suffer far more curious looks if one speaks or writes in this manner than if one were to simply use the more common pronoun *you*.

SCRAM, WHICHES: *WHICH* VERSUS *THAT*

I like to make choices simple: use *that* before a restrictive clause and *which* before everything else.

A restrictive clause can't be eliminated; it restricts the noun.

Dogs <u>that howl</u> make me crazy.

That howl restricts the kind of dogs I mean. Without it, I'd be saying all dogs make me crazy, which isn't true.

A nonrestrictive clause can be dropped without changing the meaning of the sentence.

Dogs, <u>which have four legs</u>, run fast.

All dogs run fast, so leaving out the words *which have four legs* doesn't change the meaning of the sentence.

A tip (with apologies to Wiccans and Hermione Granger) is that you can always throw out the "whiches" and no harm will be done. If it would change the meaning to throw out the clause, you need a *that*.

Throw out the whiches.

Parentheses and Abbreviations

Let's combine parentheses with abbreviations! (Oh, come on. Live a little.)

If the bit inside parentheses isn't a complete sentence and ends with an abbreviation, you put a period after the abbreviation, and another period after the parenthesis to end the sentence. You can't ignore the parenthesis and let the period end both the abbreviation and the sentence:

Squiggly likes chocolate (including chocolate mixed with yummies such as nuts, candy, etc.).

If the bit inside parentheses is a complete sentence and ends with an abbreviation, you only use one period because the final parenthesis isn't in your way.

(Squiggly likes sweets—candy, cookies, cake, etc.)

Wrap It Up: Gifting

When someone says they are *gifting* someone earrings, I resist grinding my teeth or grabbing them by the neck to squeeze.

I take a deep breath and think to myself, or perhaps note to them, that according to the *Oxford English Dictionary*, *gift* has been used as a verb for four hundred years. How interesting it is that the word had fallen out of common use for many years, and only recently experienced a revival, perhaps because accountants often speak of gifting money when they advise clients about the gift tax. *Gifting*—a linguistic "gift" newly discovered by the finance industry.

Language Rock Star: Benjamin Franklin

When you think of Benjamin Franklin you probably think of electricity, spectacles, or the Constitution, but he was also a printer and an advocate of spelling reform. Franklin created a phonetic alphabet that dropped letters he considered redundant (*c*, *j*, *q*, *w*, *x*, and *y*—even though *Benjamin* contains a *j*), and he replaced them with six new letters representing sounds not covered by the current alphabet. He went so far as to commission a type set for his alphabet. It was never adopted, but he was a contemporary of Noah Webster and is likely to have influenced Webster's successful efforts to introduce new American spellings.

Palette Versus *Palate* Versus *Pallet*

Remember that *palate*, which means the roof of your mouth or describes your sense of taste, ends with *-ate*—it's all about food. *Pallet* refers to a bed or those wooden platforms goods are strapped to for shipping. That's a little harder to remember, but think of the two *l*'s as a little rectangular bed or shipping pallet in the middle of the word. Finally, a *palette* is a set of colors or the board artists use to hold paints. There are many famous French painters (e.g., Monet, Renoir, Cézanne) and the *-ette* ending on *palette* is common in French. (My name, Mignon, actually comes from *mignonette*, a French word that is the name of a plant with small, fragrant flowers.)

WORD SCRAMBLE: IRREGULAR VERBS

The past tense forms of most English verbs end in *-ed* or *-en*. These are called regular verbs. The past tense of irregular verbs is formed with some other spelling, and you have to just memorize them. See if you can unscramble some of these common irregular verbs.

koeaw_____

ameecb_____

stouhg_____

soitomk_____

ozerf_____

The answer key is on page 212.

GRR: *GORILLA* VERSUS *GUERRILLA*

Unless you're hawking primates, you're not engaging in gorilla marketing. It's called guerrilla marketing. The term *guerrilla* comes from a Spanish word that means "little war." Guerrilla fighters typically launch small, targeted attacks as opposed to the large military campaigns run by nations. Similarly, guerrilla marketers often use targeted, creative marketing methods as opposed to the expensive, traditional campaigns run by large corporations.

Did you see the movie *Gorillas in the Mist*?

Gorillas scare me.

We hoped to save money by using guerrilla marketing.

The soldiers weren't trained for guerrilla warfare.

On Second Thought: Formatting Thoughts

Most people know that direct quotations belong within quotation marks, but how do you quote someone's thoughts?

The most common recommendation for dealing with such unspoken discourse in nonfiction writing is to use quotation marks just as you would for spoken discourse.

**"I said to myself, 'Keep fighting; don't give up,'"
Smith said.**

**According to Smith, she struggled to stay in the game,
rallying herself with the thought, "Keep fighting;
don't give up."**

If you're writing fiction and want to convey a character's thoughts, special formatting isn't necessary, but you can choose to use quotation marks or italics if it seems appropriate.

No Special Treatment
Squiggly looked at the horizon in despair.

Nobody is coming to help.

Quotation Marks
He counted his remaining chocolates.

"Nobody is coming to help," Squiggly thought.

Italics

**Squiggly looked at the horizon in despair. *Nobody is
coming to help.* He counted his remaining chocolates.
I'm going to die. He tried to remember where he'd last
seen water. *I've heard thirst is a terrible way to die.*
Panic was beginning to set in. *I don't want to die!*
Delirium would soon follow if he didn't get out of the
sun.**

PARENTHESES IN THE MIDDLE OF A SENTENCE

When a complete sentence is surrounded by parentheses in the middle of another sentence, terminal punctuation is only used if the sentence calls for a question mark or exclamation point. Keep the first letter of the first word of the parenthetical sentence lowercase:

> **I like working at Java Jungle (the art changes frequently), but Dreamers has bigger tables.**

> **Java Jungle is noisy (could they turn down the music?), so I often end up at the West Street Market.**

If the sentence ends with an abbreviation, include the period that ends the abbreviation.

> **I like Java Jungle (the atmosphere includes art, music, etc.), but the West Street Market is a better place to write.**

MIMSIES IN THE SMOG: PORTMANTEAU WORDS

Portmanteau words, also known as blends, are words such as *smog* that are made from a combination of sounds from other words, in this case *smoke* and *fog*. *Portmanteau* is French (itself a portmanteau word) for a type of suitcase that opens into two parts. Lewis Carroll assigned *portmanteau* its newer linguistic meaning in his book *Alice Through the Looking Glass* when describing the words *mimsy* (from *miserably* and *flimsy*) and *slithy* (from *slimy* and *lithe*). Other examples include *brunch* (made up of the sounds from *breakfast* and *lunch*), *spork* (from *spoon* and *fork*), and *Bennifer* (from *Ben* and *Jennifer*).

TILL VERSUS UNTIL VERSUS 'TIL

Can you till the land till the cows come home? Yes, but many people are confused about *till*, *until*, and *'til*. When you're talking about a period of time that must lapse before something happens, *till* and *until* are equivalent. Don't believe it? Check a dictionary. *Till* actually came first, and *until* followed more recently.

We spun in circles until we were dizzy.

We ran till we were breathless.

'Til is also an acceptable shortened form of *until*, but the *American Heritage Dictionary of the English Language* says the form is "etymologically incorrect."

If you want to avoid controversy, it's safest to stick with *until*.

THE HOUSE THAT GRAMMAR BUILT: PARALLEL CONSTRUCTION

Using parallel construction means making similar parts of your work follow the same pattern. When you get advice to start every section of your résumé with an action word like *created* or *achieved*, you're being advised to use parallel construction. In simple lists, you also want to make sure each part is formatted the same way:

Aardvark bought <u>a</u> tie, <u>a</u> shirt, and <u>a</u> hat. (right)

Aardvark bought <u>a</u> tie, shirt, and <u>a</u> hat. (wrong)

Squiggly wished <u>for a</u> bicycle, <u>for a</u> tent, and <u>for a</u> kite. (right)

Squiggly wished <u>for a</u> bicycle, <u>the</u> tent, and kite. (so wrong!)

Quiz: *Canceled Versus Cancelled*

In America, which is the correct spelling?

a. **The play was cancelled.**
b. **The play was canceled.**

The answer and an explanation are on page 212.

Special Order: *Specially Versus Especially*

This was an especially fun tip to write; it was specially designed for your enjoyment. Does that help you see the difference between *especially* and *specially*? *Especially* usually means "particularly," whereas *specially* usually means "in a special or careful manner" or "specifically."

This market is especially tough on retirees.

Chocolate, especially dark chocolate, was Squiggly's weakness.

Aardvark delivered the specially minted commemorative coins.

The cake had been specially prepared for the occasion.

AFFECT VERSUS EFFECT

The difference between *affect* and *effect* is actually pretty straightforward. Most of the time you use *affect* as a verb and *effect* as a noun.

To affect most commonly means something like "to influence" or "to change."

The arrows affected Aardvark.

To affect can also mean, roughly, "to act in a way you don't feel," as in *He affected an air of superiority*.

Effect has a lot of subtle meanings as a noun, but to me the meaning "a result" seems to be at the core of all the definitions.

The effect was eye-popping.

In rare instances the roles are switched, but if you remember that *affect* is for an action (both start with *a*), and you can usually put an article (*the* or *an*) in front of *effect* without ruining the sentence, you'll be right most of the time. Or you can use the example sentences in the cartoon to help you remember the difference.

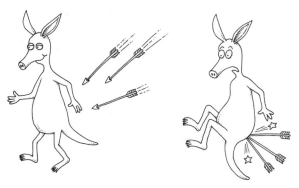

The arrows *affected* Aardvark.   The *effect* was eye-popping.

THE EXCEPTION TO THE AFFECT-IS-A-VERB-EFFECT-IS-A-NOUN RULE

As you learned yesterday, *affect* is usually a verb and *effect* is usually a noun. So what are the exceptions?

Affect can be a noun when you are talking about psychology. It means the mood that someone appears to have. Psychologists find it useful because they can never really know what someone else is feeling. Technically, they can only know how someone appears to be feeling.

He displayed a happy affect.

Effect can be a verb that essentially means "to bring about" or "to accomplish."

Aardvark hoped to effect change at the restaurant.

DIRECT AND INDIRECT QUOTATIONS

When should you put single words like *yes* and *no* in quotation marks? It depends on whether you're quoting exactly what someone said (a direct quotation) or talking about what someone said or might say (an indirect quotation).

If you are *directly* quoting someone, put the word in quotation marks.

Sarah smiled and said, "Yes."

If you are *indirectly* quoting someone, don't put the word in quotation marks.

He wondered if Sarah would say yes.

LANGUAGE ROCK STARS: THE IMMORTALS

No one body determines English language rules. Instead, the rules are "made" by lexicographers (people who write dictionaries) and various influential college handbooks and style guides such as *The Chicago Manual of Style*, *The AP Stylebook*, and the *MLA Handbook*. That's one reason English has so many style choices. But some countries do have formal language councils. Since 1635 France has had a body known as l'Académie française (the French Academy) to safeguard the French language. The forty members, known as immortals, publish an official French dictionary and aim to preserve official French, for example, by discouraging the adoption of English words such as *e-mail*.

WE USED TO HAVE MUCH MORE FUN: *USED TO* VERSUS *USE TO*

The correct phrase is *used to* with a *d* on the end. It's confusing because the *d* and *t* sounds between the words are easy to run together, making the phrase sound like *use to* when spoken aloud.

The quick and dirty tip for remembering the correct spelling is this: when you say you *used to* do something, you are talking about the past, and you make most verbs past tense by adding -*d* or -*ed* to the end. So just as you say you heav*ed* yourself into the kayak or twirl*ed* in a circle, you say you us*ed* *to* have a lot more fun.

Quiz: Oh, What a Difference It Makes

Choose the better sentence:

   a. Squiggly was different from the other snails.
   b. Squiggly was different than the other snails.

The answer and an explanation are on page 212.

Proofreading Tips

It doesn't do much good to know grammar, spelling, and punctuation rules if you get them wrong anyway because of typos. If you can't have someone else proofread your work—always the best option—wait as long as possible to proofread it yourself. That gives you time to forget what you meant to write, so you're less likely to read what you intended instead of what's actually there. Proofread on paper instead of a computer screen (so much for the paperless office), and read your work out loud to catch errors you might miss another way. And although it won't catch everything, use a spell-checker.

WORD SEARCH: FOREIGN WORDS IN ENGLISH

English borrows liberally from other languages, especially words to describe animals or foods that are introduced from other countries. This puzzle contains just a few of the words that came to English from Dutch, Spanish, French, German, Swedish, Arabic, and Persian.

The answer key is on page 213.

R	L	E	B	E	W	S	M	R	Z	Z	P
U	Z	A	A	R	E	F	A	C	E	F	T
K	W	D	E	L	C	I	H	L	Z	I	R
R	K	S	S	F	L	L	M	X	S	G	E
A	K	C	M	D	Y	I	U	I	T	A	K
V	N	H	O	T	E	B	R	G	U	L	H
D	E	A	R	U	N	U	V	R	H	Y	A
R	T	D	G	P	T	N	A	K	E	P	K
A	R	E	A	A	U	G	O	N	V	U	I
A	A	N	S	K	H	A	S	O	J	N	G
U	G	F	B	C	C	L	P	M	X	D	A
G	R	R	O	S	C	O	X	U	F	I	I
R	E	E	R	F	Y	W	X	M	L	T	V
A	D	U	D	F	R	H	G	M	A	D	C
T	N	D	N	W	E	W	N	W	Z	V	W
I	I	E	P	F	I	D	A	H	I	J	D
N	K	S	A	G	J	U	U	L	P	Q	L

AARDVARK	DAM	KAPUT	SALSA
BUNGALOW	SCHADENFREUDE	KHAKI	SMORGASBORD
CHUTNEY	GUERRILLA	KINDERGARTEN	TREK
CAFÉ	JIHAD	PUNDIT	

Tag. You're It. Question Tags.

How do you turn a statement into a question? With a question tag, of course! A question tag isn't a piece of paper you hang around a statement's neck or stick on its lapel, it's a little add-on question at the end of a statement. Question tags can make a huge difference in the tone and meaning of a sentence.

> **You remembered my birthday! (Statement. Happy.)**
>
> **You remembered my birthday, right? (Question because of the question tag *right* at the end. Hesitant or accusing.)**
>
> **He wouldn't forget my birthday. (Statement. Confident.)**
>
> **He wouldn't forget my birthday, would he? (Question. Uncertain.)**

Deep Impact

Impact has taken root in the business world as a replacement for the verbs *affect* or *influence*, as in *Cutting prices will impact our revenue*. The problem is that many people maintain that impact is only proper as a noun (*the impact was greater than expected*) and shouldn't be used as a verb. They believe the verb *impact* only means "to hit," and any other use is just irritating jargon. Yes, you'll find *impact* as a verb in the dictionary, but you'll lead a happier life if you shun such usage.

Typo Trouble, Take One

The next time you're caught in an embarrassing typo, comfort yourself with the thought that it could be worse. The central bank of Kazakhstan once misspelled *bank* on its money. One feels for them. The error arose from a transition between languages. When Kazakhstan was part of the USSR, people typically wrote in Cyrillic script, but today citizens take pride in using the Kazakh language. Yet the bank printed the notes with a Cyrillic *k* instead of a Kazakh *k*. The misprinting caused an uproar: politicians claimed the error had political undertones and were outraged when the bank decided to replace the notes slowly over time.

Sometimes Y

Many people learned that the English vowels are *a*, *e*, *i*, *o*, *u*, and sometimes *y*. (Ah, this topic takes me back to 1983 when I danced the nights away to "*AEIOU Sometimes Y*" by Ebn-Ozn!)

The reason for the "sometimes y" qualifier is that the letter *y* can be both a vowel and a consonant—it depends on the sound that *y* represents in the word. When *y* sounds like a vowel, it's a vowel; when it sounds like a consonant, it's a consonant.

Y is a vowel in *mystery*, *family*, and *dynamo*.

Y is a consonant in *yolk* and *beyond*.

Quiz: *Dragged* Versus *Drug*

Which of these common statements is considered dialect:

a. I dragged myself out of bed.
b. I drug myself out of bed.

The answer and an explanation are on page 213.

Every Day I Write the Book: *Everyday* Versus *Every Day*

Use *everyday* to talk about something ordinary or common. *Everyday* is an adjective. In the sentences below it modifies the nouns *clothes* and *dishes*.

These are my everyday clothes.

It's not a special occasion; just put out the everyday dishes.

When you break it into two words—*every day*—you're talking about how often you do something. *Every day* is an adverbial phrase. Below, it describes when or how often Noah took a picture and how often Squiggly drinks coffee.

Noah took a photo of himself every day for six years.

Squiggly drinks coffee every day.

Snowclone

Snowclone is the term coined by Glen Whitman, on the Language Log website (http://languagelog.ldc.upenn.edu), to describe "the some-assembly-required adaptable cliché frames for lazy journalists." The name comes from the fill-in-the-blank sentence *If Eskimos have N words for snow, X surely have Y words for Z*, which Whitman considered a snowclone because it isn't true (Eskimos don't, in fact, have an unusually large number of words for *snow*) and because it was overused by writers looking for a cute and easy way to make a comparison: *snow*, from this particular cliché, and *clone* from the idea that it is repeated or overused.

Other snowclones Whitman noted in his entry were:

In space, no one can hear you X.

X is the new Y.

Other snowclones noted by commentators include

Got X? (After the "Got Milk?" advertising campaign)

X-gate (After the Watergate scandal)

We put the X in(to) Y

It's generally best to avoid snowclones, since they are a form of cliché, but it's fun to take note of them in others' writing.

Snow is the new clay.

A Question Flurry

What if you have multiple questions and want to string them together?

Will you be mine today? forever?

The add-on question isn't a complete sentence, but it gets a question mark anyway. You usually don't capitalize the first letter, but the rules are vague. Some style guides say to capitalize the first letter if the questions are nearly a sentence or have sentence-like status, so you have to use your own judgment.

I don't consider *forever* to be nearly a sentence, but I may consider something like *until we're old and gray* to be nearly a sentence, which would make me consider capitalizing the first letter, *u*.

Heads Up, Seven Up

Ever since grade school games of "Heads Up, Seven Up," I've wondered if it's *head's up*, *heads-up*, or *heads up*.

For you, dear readers, I looked it up. Because the phrase means roughly "Everyone, lift your heads up and look out," it's referring to more than one head (even when you're talking to one person), so that eliminates *head's up*. The other two spellings are correct, depending on the context. As an interjection, *heads up* doesn't take a hyphen. As a noun, it does.

Heads up, everyone, the boss is on our floor. (interjection)

Aardvark gave Squiggly a *heads-up* about the peeve parade. (noun)

LANGUAGE ROCK STAR: WILLIAM ARCHIBALD SPOONER

It isn't everyone who gets a language quirk named after him! The misspeak known as a "spoonerism" is named after Reverend William Archibald Spooner, who held various positions at New College, Oxford, between 1867 and 1930. A spoonerism occurs when someone switches sounds between words. For example, Spooner may have said, "It is kisstomary to cuss the bride," instead of "It is customary to kiss the bride." It is not known whether Spooner actually uttered many of the spoonerisms that have been attributed to him, and it is believed he was unhappy with being so closely associated with language errors.

WHILING AWAY THE TIME: *ALTHOUGH* VERSUS *WHILE*

OK, what follows isn't actually a hard-and-fast rule, but it's my pet peeve, and it's my book, so I get to include it! Most sources say it's usually OK to use the subordinating conjunctions *although* and *while* interchangeably, but a few sources (including me) believe *while* should be reserved for instances that have an element of time, and *although* should be used for making a concession.

While I gather firewood, you can dig the pit.

Although we have wood and a pit, we forgot the matches.

WORD SCRAMBLE: SUBORDINATING CONJUNCTIONS

Subordinating conjunctions such as *although* and *while* come at the beginning of dependent clauses. They're great for making complex sentences, but you need to be careful that you don't use them to make sentence fragments (a topic you'll learn more about in two days). Try to unscramble these subordinating conjunctions:

ceeuabs_____

stpidee_____

htuogh_____

usnsle_____

hweveern_____

The answer key is on page 213.

IT'S GINORMOUS: *ENORMITY* VERSUS *ENORMOUSNESS*

Enormousness describes something huge, and *enormity* describes something overwhelmingly horrible. Long ago the words meant the same thing, but today they don't and people often wrongly use *enormity* when they mean *enormousness*. President Obama was chastised for doing so in his acceptance speech when he spoke of "the enormity of the task ahead of us." Most people agreed the challenges were daunting but not outrageous or ghastly.

The enormousness of the Grand Canyon routinely awes visitors.

The Civil War's enormity ensures that it will not be easily forgotten.

41

ARE YOU MISSING SOMETHING?
SENTENCE FRAGMENTS

You can make a complete sentence with just two words: *Squiggly hurried. Squiggly*, our beloved snail, is the subject and *hurried* is the verb.

A sentence fragment is a collection of words that can't stand on its own as a sentence. For example, if you leave out the subject or the verb, you have a sentence fragment:

No Subject
Ran to the store.

No Verb
Squiggly to the store.

Those were pretty obviously not sentences, but longer fragments can trick you. This is also a fragment:

Running to the store in the rain.

Even trickier, there is also a case where you have a subject and a verb, but you still don't have a complete sentence. Ack! You can accidentally turn a sentence into a fragment by putting a subordinating conjunction in front of it.

Because Squiggly hurried.

By adding *because*, I've messed up the sentence; now I need something to explain the *because*. The *because* makes the whole thing a dependent clause that can't exist on its own. (Well, it can exist, but it's a fragment and that's usually bad.) The dependent clause now only makes sense if it has a main clause, for example, *Aardvark was relieved because Squiggly hurried.*

Fragments have a place in writing, for example, when you're being conversational or want to add emphasis, but don't write them accidentally.

QUOTATION MARKS, PERIODS, AND COMMAS

I'm willing to bet that half of you don't know whether to put periods and commas inside or outside quotation marks. And do you know why you're confused? It's those #@(*&%$ people on the other side of the pond—no matter which side of the pond you're on—because it's done differently in Britain and America. So, if you're regularly reading CNN.com and BBC.co.uk, for example, you'll regularly see it done differently. Here's my U.S.-centric memory trick:

Inside the United States, periods and commas go inside the quotation marks. ("Jump in the pond.")

Outside the United States, periods and commas go outside the quotation marks. ("Jump in the pond".)

THERE'S A NAME FOR THAT? EUPHEMISM

Often, when you don't want to say something bad or upsetting, you use a euphemism. For example, "polite" ways to say someone has died range from the oddly consumerist *expired* to the more metaphysical *passed on*. Euphemisms sometimes result from superstition rather than politeness. For example, in the *Harry Potter* books, wary characters refer to the villain Voldemort as *He-Who-Must-Not-Be-Named*. Politicians also employ euphemisms to sway public opinion. If they call torture *enhanced interrogation techniques*, people won't object, they posit. Often, naming something that has taken on a euphemism is seen as a bold or brave move or a way of shaking off repression.

An Elusive Tip: *Allude* Versus *Elude*

Allude and *elude* may sound alike, and they come from the same Latin root meaning "to play"; but other than that, they don't have much in common. *Allude* means "to refer to indirectly." *Elude* means "to avoid capture."

The butler had alluded to a secret exit.

We hoped we could find the secret exit so we could elude the police.

A quick and dirty tip is to remember that *elude* and *escape* both start with the letter *e*.

Ack! Oof! Hello? One-Word Sentences

Last Sunday I explained that sentences need a subject and a verb, but did you catch that I used the word **usually**? In some cases, you can make a sentence with just one word. They're called imperative sentences, and they contain a single verb.

Run!

Stay.

Go!

Imperative sentences are commands, and the subject is always assumed to be the person you are talking to. If Squiggly looks at Aardvark and says, "Run!" Aardvark knows that he's the one who should be running. It's such a strong command that he knows it is imperative for him to run.

You can also make a one-word sentence using an exclamation:

Ouch!

Eureka!

QUIZ: LET'S BE REASONABLE

Place these sentences in order from worst to best.

> **a. The reason I love grammar is because it brings order to chaos.**
>
> **b. The reason I love grammar is that it brings order to chaos.**
>
> **c. I love grammar because it brings order to chaos.**

The answer and an explanation are on page 213.

MORE IMPORTANT VERSUS MORE IMPORTANTLY

You may occasionally hear or read an objection to the phrase *more importantly*. Ignore it (unless you're writing a cover letter or some other document where you'll be judged without the chance to defend yourself). *More important* and *more importantly* are both grammatically acceptable and have been in use for decades, with *more importantly* probably being the older form. The *Oxford English Dictionary Supplement* calls *more important* "a kind of sentence adjective" and *more importantly* "a kind of sentence adverb" and "a quasi-adjective." The only difference is that you have to use *more* or *most* when you use *important*, but you can use *importantly* alone.

Lie Down, Sally: *Lay* Versus *Lie*

You know you shouldn't take grammar advice from popular music, right? Music is kind of like poetry: the writers get to break the rules for artistic reasons—to create a certain effect or simply to show how rebellious they are. (At least I hope that is why there are so many grammatically incorrect songs. I'd like to believe the artists actually know the rules and choose to break them.) So, knowing that lyrics are often wrong, it shouldn't surprise you that "Lay, Lady, Lay" by Bob Dylan and "Lay Down Sally" by Eric Clapton use the wrong word. People *lie* down, to lie is to recline, so those songs should have been "Lie, Lady, Lie" and "Lie Down Sally." They probably used *lay* because *lie* has such negative connotations in its other meaning—to tell an untruth. *Lay* is what happens to objects. You lay a dollar in the musician's open guitar case. Just remember this cynical memory trick: people lie. They tell lies, and they lie around. They lie on the couch, they lie on the bed, they lie on the floor.

Aardvark is *lying* on the couch. Squiggly is *laying* the quilt on Aardvark.

Now I Lay Me Down to Sleep

If you remember the tip from yesterday, you'll remember that people lie down, they don't lay down. So why in the heck does that children's prayer read, "Now I *lay* me down to sleep"? Because *lie* doesn't take an object, and *lay* does. The prayer is written so that you are the object of your own action. When you lay a pillow on the bed, the pillow is clearly the object because it's a thing you can hold in your hands and subsequently lay down. But it also works metaphorically—when you lay yourself down, you are the object that you are laying down.

Conjugating *Lay* and *Lie*

Lay and *lie* get even trickier when you conjugate them because *lay* is the past tense of *lie*. Here's a handy chart to cut out, laminate, and keep in your wallet for conjugation emergencies.

Present	Present Participle	Past	Past Participle
Lie	Lying	Lay	Lain
Lay	Laying	Laid	Laid

Language Rock Stars: John Bangsund

Before there was Hartman's Law of Prescriptivist Retaliation, there was Muphry's Law (a play on Murphy's Law), described by Australian editor John Bangsund in a 1992 article in the *Society of Editors Newsletter*:

    a. if you write anything criticizing editing or proofreading, there will be a fault of some kind in what you have written;

    b. if an author thanks you in a book for your editing or proofreading, there will be mistakes in the book;

    c. the stronger the sentiment expressed in (a) and (b), the greater the fault;

    d. any book devoted to editing or style will be internally inconsistent.

Now you, and I, have a "law" to cite when things go wrong.

Mixed Quotation Marks

Should a question mark be placed inside or outside quotation marks? The answer varies, depending on what the quotation marks are surrounding.

If the quoted text is a question, put the question mark *inside* the quotation mark.

    Squiggly asked, "<u>Where are the fish?</u>"

If the quoted text is only part of a longer question, put the question mark *outside* the quotation mark.

    <u>Aardvark, where are the "yummies"?</u>

I remember this rule by remembering that the question mark belongs with the question—not the quotation marks. The rule is the same for exclamation points.

Quiz: Quoth the Raven

Which of the following is technically incorrect?

a. Did you send me the quotes from Stephen Colbert?
b. Did you send me the quotations from Stephen Colbert?

The answer and an explanation are on page 213.

Are You Done with That Dessert? *Done* Versus *Finished*

When you've said, "I'm done," someone has probably corrected you with a snotty little phrase like "A turkey is done; you're finished." (I've always wondered if the phrase "Stick a fork in me; I'm done" came from this same belief.) That was, indeed, the rule until about the mid-twentieth century, but usage has changed, and today nearly all major language commentators (and dictionaries) believe it's fine to apply *done* to things other than food. But watch out for those sticklers who haven't kept up with the times and still want to chase you around with a fork for doing it "wrong."

WORD SEARCH:
HOMONYMS AND HOMOPHONES

Words that sound alike but are spelled differently can be tricky for people learning English. Heck, sometimes they're tricky for people who speak only English! Technically, such words are homophones, but they are more often called homonyms. See if you can find all the commonly confusing word pairs below. Each word is distinct in the puzzle. For example, you will find *hear* separately, not as part of *shear*.

The answer key is on page 214.

Y	V	L	T	E	E	R	C	S	I	D	L	H
U	H	O	D	E	R	I	E	R	B	R	T	G
W	I	A	I	R	W	E	O	L	U	A	T	S
D	G	U	F	A	I	R	H	N	N	O	G	P
I	R	Z	X	B	L	B	U	T	A	B	Y	C
S	E	I	H	X	M	J	P	K	R	X	Y	K
C	R	C	E	Z	I	B	Z	R	A	E	H	S
R	Z	A	Z	H	S	K	F	F	F	N	Y	U
E	N	M	E	E	T	E	R	J	F	X	Q	S
T	E	H	N	H	S	M	Y	E	B	E	A	R
E	G	Z	P	S	U	B	O	U	E	K	F	R
N	X	B	U	A	R	O	U	O	H	H	T	O
A	M	O	J	Z	B	E	R	M	S	K	S	D
O	M	R	E	J	N	Q	E	N	Z	E	E	S
L	R	E	L	O	Q	Z	T	S	Q	P	N	H
E	T	D	L	S	H	E	R	E	F	A	R	E
U	X	Y	Z	X	U	S	Z	H	R	P	Y	V

BARE	DISCRETE	LOAN	SHEER
BEAR	FAIR	LONE	THEIR
BOARD	FARE	MOOSE	THERE
BORED	HEAR	MOUSSE	YOUR
DISCREET	HERE	SHEAR	YOU'RE

THE SINGLE LIFE: SINGLE QUOTATION MARKS

Single quotation marks show up when you are quoting someone who is quoting someone else. Enclose the primary speaker's comments in double quotation marks, and enclose the statement they are quoting in single quotation marks.

> **"Squiggly saved my life when he said, 'Look out!' "**
> **said Aardvark Blueback, resident of the forest.**

Single quotation marks are also sometimes used when there's a direct quotation in a headline and to highlight words with special meaning in certain disciplines such as philosophy, theology, and linguistics.

I PRESUME YOU WANT TO KNOW THIS TIP: *ASSUME* VERSUS *PRESUME*

I presume you'd like to know the difference between *assume* and *presume*.

If you *assume* something, you're basing your information on nothing—no facts, just your belief gathered from thin air.

> **Assuming she would hate him, Aardvark wouldn't**
> **ask the waitress for more coffee.**

But if you *presume* to know something, that presumption is based on evidence or facts. The explorer Sir Henry Morton Stanley uttered, "Dr. Livingstone, I presume," because he was expecting to find Dr. Livingstone.

> **After seeing the telltale footprints leading from**
> **Squiggly's room to the freezer, Aardvark presumed it**
> **was Squiggly who had taken the last ice cream bar.**

Everyone Is Happy

Everyone sounds like a lot of people, and often it is, but when you're writing a sentence, *everyone* is treated as singular. The same is true for *anyone*, *nobody*, *someone*, and other such words (which are called indefinite pronouns).

Each is also an indefinite pronoun and treated as singular. Watch out because it can be especially tricky when it's followed by a prepositional phrase with a plural noun. In such cases, it's still singular. Ignore the prepositional phrase when choosing the verb.

Each <u>of the students</u> is signing up for art.

Singular or Plural?

Did yesterday's tip make your head spin? Let's look at some specific examples combining a phrase like *one of the* or *each of the* with a plural noun. In most such sentences, an indefinite pronoun is singular and you ignore the plural part that follows.

<u>One</u> of the boys <u>spins</u> in circles.

<u>Each</u> of the girls <u>looks</u> confused.

The tricky part is when you add *who* or *that* to the mix:

Squiggly is one of the <u>snails</u> who <u>talk</u>.

In that sentence, the plural word *snails* (not the singular word *one*) is the antecedent of *who*, so you use the plural verb.

Quiz: *Comprise* Versus *Compose*

Which sentences are incorrect?

    a. Squiggly's candle collection comprises beeswax candles, soy wax candles, and cheap candles made of things he doesn't like to think about.

    b. Squiggly's candle collection is comprised of beeswax candles, soy wax candles, and cheap candles made of things he doesn't like to think about.

    c. Squiggly's candle collection is composed of beeswax candles, soy wax candles, and cheap candles made of things he doesn't like to think about.

    d. Squiggly's candle collection composes beeswax candles, soy wax candles, and cheap candles made of things he doesn't like to think about.

The answer and an explanation are on page 214.

A Capital Idea: *Capital* Versus *Capitol*

When the noun *capitol* ends with an *ol*, it's referring to buildings—state capitol buildings or the Capitol building in Washington, D.C. You can remember that the rotunda of the D.C. Capitol building is round like the letter *o*.

Capital refers to (among other things) uppercase letters, wealth, or a city that is the seat of government for its region or is important in some way. Don't get confused by the fact that *capital* with an *al* is used for a capital city and *capitol* with an *ol* is used for a capitol building. Just remember the *o* is round like a building's rotunda.

It's No Longer Trendy: Capitalizing Nouns

Between roughly 1600 and 1800 it was common to capitalize all English nouns. But today, only proper nouns get capitalized.

Proper nouns name specific things; they are usually a person's name, like *Squiggly*, or the name of a specific thing such as the *Golden Gate Bridge* or *Nobel Peace Prize*.

Common nouns are generic; they are words such as *snail*, *bridge*, and *prize*, and they don't get capitalized.

Think of common nouns as commoners: they don't get any special treatment; they aren't capitalized. Think of proper nouns as proper royalty: they get special treatment; they are capitalized.

Although you see it done a lot, it is not OK to capitalize words just to make them seem more important.

Our Salespeople deserve an Award. (wrong)

Our salespeople deserve an award. (right)

A proper noun is capitalized and names a specific person, place, or thing.

The Hoity-Toity Capital: Capitalizing *Capitol*

Last week I wrote about the difference between *capital* and *capitol*. Did you notice that sometimes I capitalized the word *capitol* and sometimes I didn't?

In the United States, *capitol* is only capitalized when it refers to the Capitol building in Washington, D.C., or a neighborhood name, such as Capitol Hill.

President Obama walked to the Capitol.

Real estate prices on Seattle's Capitol Hill are rising.

When you're writing about the capitol building of a state, *capitol* is lowercased. The states are like Rodney Dangerfield: they get no respect (or at least no capital letter)!

Wisconsin's capitol building in Madison has a classic dome.

Stand and Deliver: *Lectern* Versus *Podium*

Public speaking is scary enough without having to worry about what to call that thing you're standing on or behind. Give yourself plenty of time to prepare, and remind yourself to breathe and make eye contact without being creepy. Then proceed to the *podium* (the raised platform where speakers stand; remember that it has the same root word as *podiatrist* and it's what you put your feet on) and put your notes on the *lectern* (the stand for your papers; think of it as putting your lecture on the lectern). (In North America, *podium* is sometimes used to mean *lectern*, but it's better to stick with *lectern*.)

The Pineapple of Politeness: Malapropisms

Malapropism comes from a French phrase meaning "badly for the purpose." It came into popular use to describe the silly misuse of words after the playwright Richard Sheridan named one of his characters, who had a habit of ridiculously mixing up words, Mrs. Malaprop.

Malapropisms occur when someone substitutes a similar-sounding word for another word. For example, George W. Bush was reported to say "nuclear power pants" instead of "nuclear power plants" in 2003 and, in Sheridan's play *The Rivals*, Mrs. Malaprop said, "He's the very pineapple of politeness" instead of "He's the very pinnacle of politeness."

Settle Down, You Crazy Verbs! Gerunds

As if there weren't enough nouns, someone had to invent a way to make more.

Take a verb and add -*ing* to the end. What do you get? A noun! If you want to know the fancy name for it, a verb that's been converted to a noun by adding -*ing* to the end is called a gerund.

For example, take the verb *act*. Add -*ing* to the end and you get a noun—a profession, acting.

Squiggly likes to <u>act</u>. (verb)

<u>Acting</u> is not as easy as it looks. (gerund)

It works with other verbs, too:

Aardvark <u>sings</u> in the shower. (verb)

Aardvark's <u>singing</u> almost deafened Squiggly. (gerund)

Word Scramble: Quash the Qualifiers

People often overuse qualifiers—those unnecessary modifiers, such as *a bit* and *sort of*, that don't add much to what they are describing. Try to unscramble the common qualifiers below and then weed them out of your writing.

tallycua_____

titlel_____

yetprt_____

layrel_____

hetrar_____

The answer key is on page 214.

Bend Over Backward: *Backward* Versus *Backwards*

In the United States, the correct choice is *backward*, not *backwards*, whether you're using the word as an adjective or as an adverb.

I bend over backward to make you happy. (adverb)

Consumers hope for backward compatibility in software. (adjective)

The reason you may be confused is that it is different in British English, so if you read the BBC website, for example, you'll see *backwards* as an adverb and *backward* as an adjective.

The story is similar for *toward*: it's *toward* in the United States and *towards* in Britain. With both of these words, you can remember the correct U.S. spelling by thinking that Americans like shortcuts, so we've lopped off the *s*.

LIST MANIA! FORMATTING VERTICAL LISTS

Bullets are just big dots used to highlight list items when their order doesn't matter. I usually list the items alphabetically or in some other way that makes sense. For example, in marketing materials, put your most important product feature or selling point first:

- **Save money**
- **Save water**
- **Grow vegetables**
- **Impress your neighbors**

Use numbered lists when the items must follow a specific sequence, for example, to list the stepwise tasks that are required—in order—to start up a piece of machinery:

1. **Plug in**
2. **Turn on power switch**
3. **Release safety latch**
4. **Tilt toward the Death Star**

Finally, letters are useful when you're implying that readers need to choose individual items or when items don't need to follow a specific sequence, but you want to refer to them again later. Choose the correct answer:

a. **Pizza**
b. **Chocolate**
c. **Broccoli**
d. **Rhubarb**

COLONS

In sentences, colons only go after something that could stand as a sentence on its own. Never use a colon after a sentence fragment. This is a correct example because the part before the colon could be a complete sentence by itself: *Squiggly has two pets: Fluffy and Rascal.*

A quick and dirty tip is that, most of the time, if you can replace a colon with the word *namely*, then the colon is the right choice. For example, you could say *Squiggly has two pets, namely, Fluffy and Rascal.* Nevertheless, there are also instances where you can use a colon and *namely* doesn't work. For example, *The band was wildly popular: they sold out the Coliseum.*

CAPITALIZING NAMES OF DEGREES

People often think there is a typo on my "About Grammar Girl" Web page because it says I have an undergraduate degree in English (capitalized) and a graduate degree in biology (lowercased).

Although I've never claimed to be perfect, that isn't a typo. *English* is capitalized because it's derived from a proper noun (England), and *biology* is lowercased because it is not derived from a proper noun. Similarly, *Spanish*, *Italian*, and *German* are capitalized because they are derived from the country names *Spain*, *Italy*, and *Germany*; *chemistry*, *math*, and *visual arts* are not capitalized because they don't come from proper nouns.

Lend Me Your Ears: *Loan* Versus *Lend*

In the United Kingdom, *lend* is the verb and *loan* is the noun. A memory trick is to remember that *loan* and *noun* both have *o*'s in them, and *lend* and *verb* both have *e*'s in them.

In the United States, most language experts consider the words interchangeable when you are talking about money or items. Nevertheless, some sticklers disagree, and if you wish to avoid their ire, you should stick to the U.K. rules.

> **Squiggly asked Aardvark to lend him money and a bike.**

> **Aardvark gave Squiggly a loan of money but wouldn't part with his bike.**

Who's Your Friend Again? As Well As Versus And

When you put something after *as well as* you're saying it's not as important as something you'd put after *and*.

> **Squiggly and Aardvark are at the store. (Read this as "Two beings we care about equally, Squiggly and Aardvark, are at the store.")**

> **Squiggly as well as Aardvark is at the store. (Read this as "Squiggly is at the store, and some guy we don't care about very much named Aardvark went with him.")**

> **Britney Spears as well as her assistant is at the store.**

Note that using *and* creates a compound subject that needs a plural verb, and using *as well as* leaves the important subject singular, so it takes a singular verb.

Quiz: Apostrophe Madness

Which is correct?

a. do's and don't's
b. dos and don'ts
c. dos' and don'ts'

The answer and an explanation are on page 214.

Like a Rock: Metaphor Versus Simile

Metaphors and similes add color to writing and can help you get a point across by comparing something foreign or complex to something familiar to your reader. For example, to explain how chemicals make genes, you might write:

The four chemical bases are <u>like</u> letters, and genes are <u>like</u> words made from those four letters.

Those examples are similes because they compare one thing to another; they use the word *like*.

Metaphors are different. They claim something actually *is* something else. They don't use words such as *like* or *as*:

Chemical bases <u>are</u> the building blocks of genes.

GRIPPING DIALOGUE:
INTRODUCING A QUOTATION: COMMAS

The most common way to introduce a short quotation is with a comma.

Aardvark said, "Ho, mighty peeves, enter my trap."

When the attribution follows the quotation, replace the terminal punctuation mark with a comma, unless it's a question mark or exclamation point.

"We're not quite that stupid," said the head peeve.

"Do you really think we're that stupid?" asked the second in command.

When you introduce a quotation with a word such as *that* or *with*, thereby making the quotation part of your sentence, don't use a comma.

Aardvark knew that Section 4 of the *Peeve Avenger Manual* begins with "Peeves are even more stupid than they look."

Aardvark said, "Ho, mighty peeves, enter my trap."

Must You Be So Formal? Introducing a Quotation: Colons

When you have a quotation that is at least one complete sentence, you may opt to introduce it with a colon, which is a stronger and more formal introductory element than a comma. Writers often choose to use colons when introducing particularly long quotations.

Aardvark wrote: "Long live Aardvark, avenger of good grammar, enemy of the peeves, known throughout the land as the Great Bluebacked Warrior."

Even when introducing quotations, it's important to remember that a colon only follows something that could be a complete sentence on its own.

Because he was feeling grandiose: "Oh, ho!" (Wrong because the colon is after a fragment and the quotation is too short for an introductory colon.)

Wake Up and Smell the Coffee on the Wall: Mixed Metaphors

A metaphor is when you use something familiar to explain something else. Sports metaphors tend to be popular, and they're also easy to mix. A sports metaphor is something like telling your employees *It's our turn at bat* when it's time to give a presentation. You're comparing work to baseball. But be careful: if you said, "It's our turn at bat, so let's make a touchdown for the company," you'd have mixed baseball and football metaphors, and your employees wouldn't know whether to put themselves on a metaphorical baseball field or football field.

Mondegreens

Mondegreens are errors of the ears—the mishearing of something, usually a song lyric, so that a new meaning is created. For example, in "Jingle Bells" people have reported mishearing the lyric "Bells on bobtail ring" as "Bells on Bob's tail ring."

The name *mondegreen* was coined by a writer named Sylvia Wright who, as a youth, misheard the last line from a seventeenth-century Scottish ballad as "And Lady Mondegreen" instead of "And laid him on the green."

> **They hae slain the Earl of Murray,**
> **And laid him on the green.**

Wright, with the wild imagination of a child, made up an elaborate backstory for the devoted "Lady Mondegreen" before discovering her error.

Make Your Alma Mater Proud: Graduated

For some reason, it's becoming more common for people to misuse the word *graduated*. Every year around June, people start sending me messages complaining about relatives or neighbors bragging about how their sweet child graduated high school or college. Most grammarians say such a construction is incorrect because a school does the act of graduating students, so students are graduated *from* a school.

> **Stanford graduated thousands of students this year.**

> **Sandy graduated from Stanford.**

If you want to be persnickety, you can also say a student was graduated from a school:

> **Sandy was graduated from Stanford.**

Quiz: *And* Versus *To*

Which sentence is correct?

a. Make sure and download every song I want.

b. Make sure to download every song I want.

The answer and an explanation are on page 214.

A Versus *An*

Many people were taught to use *a* before words that start with consonants and *an* before words that start with vowels, but it's actually not that simple. What matters is not the first letter of the word but the first sound of the word. *M*, for example, can stand for a consonant sound or a vowel sound, so *a* goes before some words that start with *m* and *an* goes before others:

Squiggly wanted a mustard sandwich.

Squiggly wanted an M.B.A.

Other letters that can go either way include *h* (a horse, an honor), *u* (a Utopian, an uncle), and *o* (a one, an oar).

WORD SEARCH: THEY SURE TALK FUNNY EVERYWHERE BUT HERE: REGIONALISMS

Every region has its own sayings. You can use them to add color to your fiction writing, but be careful about using them in nonfiction writing. In many areas they aren't considered standard English or can be distracting if you use words that aren't local where your work is published. See if you can find all the common regionalisms below. The words are in groups that mean the same thing in different regions.

The answer key is on page 215.

J	H	O	A	G	Y	B	W	H	T	R	I	N
Q	T	S	N	I	Y	L	S	E	E	Q	G	S
Z	R	Z	B	P	H	I	S	L	P	O	P	Z
K	E	G	O	C	D	Q	O	T	E	G	F	S
O	X	M	U	T	E	R	Q	U	S	V	S	R
V	G	O	O	K	E	Y	F	O	U	L	O	D
Y	C	H	A	S	V	R	Z	B	O	L	D	U
J	P	H	S	K	A	S	S	A	Y	A	A	B
Y	S	A	L	P	U	C	C	D	P	Y	A	F
E	C	V	P	B	R	E	D	N	I	R	G	O
V	W	E	L	C	Z	P	O	U	Z	V	F	B
R	E	P	O	Z	C	E	T	O	Z	B	H	V
O	T	K	S	F	I	G	R	R	A	N	E	G
T	E	D	A	V	E	N	P	O	R	T	R	W
A	N	E	O	H	Z	U	D	U	G	J	O	W
R	U	B	I	A	F	O	S	Q	M	L	F	D
Y	I	N	V	P	P	L	E	G	Q	L	Z	K

YALL	COKE	PIZZA	HOAGY	ROUNDABOUT
YOUSE	COUCH	PIE	HERO	ROTARY
YINS	SOFA	FRAPPE	GRINDER	
SODA	DAVENPORT	SHAKE	CASSEROLE	
POP	LOUNGE	SUB	HOTDISH	

Dear, Sweet Semicolon: The Basics

Ah, the semicolon. I love it so. It helps you express complex, related thoughts; and so few people know how to use it, it makes me feel smart when I throw it in a sentence. Writers have both lamented its decline and called for its banishment, which gives it an endearing underdog's glamour. Most commonly, semicolons join sentences that could stand on their own and serve to cement a relationship between the two thoughts.

Semicolons are underdogs; I find them endearing.

It's wrong to use semicolons to join sentences that aren't related in some way:

Semicolons are underdogs; I ate chicken for lunch. (wrong)

Should I Make Up a Grammar Award? Capitalizing Award Names

Everyone likes to win awards, but do you know how to write about them? Formal award names (such as Oscar, Grammy, Nobel Prize, and Pulitzer Prize) are capitalized because they are proper nouns—the name of something specific. General award terms are not capitalized when they are used descriptively.

Who will win a Pulitzer Prize this year?

Amy Winehouse won five Grammys.

Doris Lessing won a Nobel Prize.

The *Los Angeles Times* won a journalism prize.

Amy Winehouse is an award-winning musician.

Doris Lessing won a literature prize.

It's Super Best:
Comparatives Versus Superlatives

Words such as *better*, *more*, and *taller* are called comparatives, and you use them when you are comparing two things. Words such as *best*, *most*, and *tallest* are called superlatives, and you use them when you are comparing more than two things.

You have chocolate and apple pie? I think chocolate is better.

Oh, now you have chocolate, apple, and strawberry pie? I still think chocolate is best.

The quick and dirty tip is to remember comparatives are for two things because *comparative* has the sound *pair* in it.

Spectacularer? When to Use More
and When to Add -ER

Have you ever found yourself wondering "Should I say something is *more heavy* or *heavier*"?

If you're dealing with a one-syllable word, you almost always add an *-er* or *-est* suffix.

That tree was taller than I expected.

He picked the tallest trees in the nursery.

There are a few irregular exceptions. For example, only your two-year-old niece would say *gooder* and *badder*. You should say *better* and *worse*.

On the other hand, if your word is three syllables or longer, you almost always put *more* or *most* in front.

That was the most spectacular tip in the book.

Quiz: *Sort* Versus *Kind* Versus *Type*

Which of the following is correct?

a. I like this kind of chocolate.
b. I like this type of chocolate.
c. I like this sort of chocolate.

The answer and an explanation are on page 215.

Pronunciation Perils: *The* ("thuh") Versus *The* ("thee")

Did you know there are two ways to pronounce *the*? The rules are like those for when to use *a* and *an*—it depends on the first sound in the following word—but unlike *a* versus *an*, the difference is in how you pronounce the word. If the word following *the* starts with a consonant sound, you pronounce *the* as "thuh." If the word following *the* starts with a vowel sound, you pronounce *the* as "thee."

Did he bring "thuh" cheese platter?

Where is "thuh" universal remote?

I prefer "thee" effervescent water.

Did she get "thee" MRI?

I Wish There Were Fewer Things to Remember: Less Versus Fewer

Less and *fewer* are easy to mix up. They mean the same thing—the opposite of *more*—but you use them differently: you use *less* with mass nouns and *fewer* with count nouns.

A count noun is something you can count. On my desk, I see books and M&M's. I can count those things, so they are count nouns and the right word to use is *fewer*.

I should eat fewer M&M's.

Mass nouns are things you can't count individually. Again, on my desk I see tape and clutter. These things can't be counted, so the right word to use is *less*.

If I had less clutter, my desk would be cleaner.

I remember when to use *less* and *fewer* by thinking of Aardvark fishing in a lake. The water is low in the lake this year, so there is less water in the lake. *Less* and *lake* both begin with the letter *l*. Squiggly is worried that Aardvark won't catch enough fish for dinner. "We'll have fewer fish for dinner," Squiggly thinks fretfully. *Fewer* and *fish* both start with the letter *f*.

There is *less* water in the lake. We'll have *fewer* fish for dinner.

Semicolons with Conjunctions

Last Monday I showed you how to splice together sentences with semicolons, but they have another use. Semicolons can step in to clear things up when a sentence gets overwhelmed by commas. For example, normally you'd separate items in a list with commas, but if your list items themselves need commas, you separate them with semicolons:

Aardvark brought meat, cheese, and wine; Sir Fragalot brought wood, paper, and matches; and Squiggly brought chocolate.

Semicolons also work with conjunctions to join sentences when the first sentence contains commas:

If you come, Squiggly will be happy; and I will feed you wine, cheese, and chocolate.

Exceptions to the Rules about *Less* and *Fewer*

There are exceptions to the rule that *less* is only for things you can't count. For example, although you can count time, money, and distance, they can also be divided into infinitely small units, which makes them more like mass nouns, so you use the word *less*.

The reception lasted less than two hours.

I hope the band charged less than $400.

The rate of return fell to less than $1.9854 per share.

So remember, most of the time *fewer* is for things you can count and *less* is for things you can't count; but even though you can count time, money, and distance, they call for *less*.

Language Rock Star: James Parton, Dictionary Warrior

Dictionaries are viewed by many as the final law on word usage. Therefore, the reaction to dictionaries (and changes to them) is shockingly passionate. Take James Parton's reaction to the publication of *Webster's Third International Dictionary* in 1961, which many at the time felt was wildly permissive. Parton, the publisher of *American Heritage* magazine, first tried to buy a controlling interest in the dictionary's publisher, the G. and C. Merriam Company, so he could pull the dictionary from the market. When that strategy failed, he instigated the publishing of a competing, more traditional and prescriptive dictionary. Yes, the *American Heritage Dictionary* and its usage panel exist because of passions over perceived intolerable faults in *Webster's Third*.

Come One, Come All: These Ones

The word *ones* can be plural, as in *I like the red ones*. You could even say *I like these red ones*. Imagine that *ones* is standing in for the word *roses* or *apples*. But *I like these ones* is redundant and incorrect. *These* is already standing in for the noun. You should just say *I like these*.

The situation is the same with *those*:

He likes those ones. (redundant)

He likes those. (better)

The phrases *this one* and *that one* don't seem to bother linguists, but it doesn't hurt to take a second look when you use the phrases to make sure you aren't being unnecessarily wordy.

WORD SCRAMBLE: PIECES AND PARTS

Traditionally, words can be placed into eight different categories. See if you can unscramble those parts of speech below.

nuno_____

ponnrou_____

revb_____

decjatvie_____

badrev_____

tiispoonrep_____

toojinnnucc_____

jetirecointn_____

The answer key is on page 215.

IRONICAL

This may surprise you, but *ironical* is a real word. It is an alternative adjective form of *irony* and it means the same thing as *ironic*. *Ironical* is the more old-fashioned form of the word, and *ironic* is the most common form in use today. You can choose to use either one, but people are more likely to look at you funny if you use *ironical*. (It is more common to hear *ironical* in Britain than in America.)

It's ironic that he wrote his most famous opera after he became deaf.

It's ironical that he wrote his most famous opera after he became deaf.

Isn't It Ironic?

Whether you want to say something is ironic or ironical, you need to use the word in the proper situation, and that's tricky. Irony is one of those things that's difficult to define, but you know it when you see it. What's ironic in one situation or to one person is not necessarily ironic in all situations or to all people because irony is related to the expected outcome or behavior.

Irony is when something is the opposite of what you expect or what the speaker means. It's ironic when environmentalists fly around the world (using energy) to encourage people to use less energy. It's not ironic if a pilot flies a lot. If Squiggly sees the rain and says, "I can't wait to go outside," he's being ironic because he doesn't mean what he's saying. It wouldn't be ironic if he did love rain.

Irony can also be visual. A few days ago I saw a big, burly biker wearing a pink hat with pom-poms (oh, for a camera!). I assume he was being ironic and was wearing the hat because it's exactly the opposite of what people would expect him to wear. The hat would not have been ironic on a thirteen-year-old girl. Another kind of irony is when actors in a play are portrayed as blind to the circumstances around them, but the audience knows.

A common mistake is to treat an unhappy coincidence as irony. It isn't ironic that your oven breaks on Thanksgiving morning or you run into your old boyfriend at the café where you used to hang out together.

That's Kansas' Statute to You! Making Words That End in *s* Possessive

You probably won't believe me because everyone learns this one way or the other as a rule, but whether you add another *s* with the apostrophe to make words that end with *s* possessive is a style choice. For example, *The Elements of Style* recommends adding the *s* (*James's*), *The AP Stylebook* recommends leaving it off (*James'*). U.S. Supreme Court justices have squabbled about it, with David Souter championing *Kansas's* and Clarence Thomas backing *Kansas'*. Some people use the even more confusing rule that you add the *s* if you pronounce it and leave it off if you don't, which would give us *King Ramses' tomb*, but *Charles's sons*. I prefer to use a lone apostrophe.

Hey, Baby

Nicknames are capitalized, but terms of endearment are not. The difference is that a nickname is a specific, alternative name for someone, whereas a term of endearment can be used for anyone; it's not specific to an individual.

It's you and me, baby.

Nobody puts Baby in a corner.

The same concept applies to family names such as *mother*, *mom*, *father*, *dad, aunt, uncle*, and *cousin*: the words are only capitalized if they are being used as part of someone's name.

Say hi to your mother.

Say hi to Mom.

Did you call Aunt Mathilda?

My aunt, Mathilda, always hiccups during dinner.

Faux Pas? Foreign Words and Redundancy

Using foreign words can tempt people into redundancy to make their meaning clear. Take the phrase *chai tea*. It's redundant because *chai* is the Hindi word for "tea."

Marketers could create campaigns that explain the foreign word's meaning—try our chai: a delicious tea made with milk, sugar, and spices—but space is often limited in stores and on signs, so it's not surprising that the concept gets shortened to *chai tea*. As a result, in America the phrase *chai tea* comes to mean a particular kind of tea made in the Indian style. If you wish to avoid redundancy, just ask for chai.

Movement of the People: *People* Versus *Persons*

Nowadays, *people* is almost always the right choice when you are talking about more than one person.

Some dictionaries don't even include *persons* as the plural of *person* anymore, and the few dictionaries that do include *persons* note that it is uncommon, archaic, or going out of style. Traditionally, *people* was proper when referring to a mass of people (e.g., Squiggly couldn't believe how many people were at the wrestling match), and *persons* was proper when referring to a distinct number of individuals (e.g., Squiggly noted that eight persons showed up for the book club meeting).

Quiz: Loosy Goosy: *Loose* Versus *Lose*

Some people have a hard time remembering the difference between *loose* and *lose*. Can you choose the correct sentence?

a. She'd lost so much weight her pants were loose.
b. Don't loose your keys!

The answer and an explanation are on page 215.

Blah, Blah, Blah: Wordiness

Wordiness bugs people. If you don't believe me, I'd be happy to show you the gazillion e-mail messages I get from listeners on this topic. (See page 159, Tuesday.) These complaints are often laced with venom. It's as if the complainer has been locked in a box and forced to listen to the same wordy phrase over and over, again and again. (Oh, wait, isn't that the definition of cubicle life?) In fact, the phrases *over and over* and *again and again* are a form of wordiness. Wordiness is evil—it creeps into your writing and it appears in many forms, including unnecessary words; repeating phrases, words, or thoughts; and overwriting. Avoid it unless you want someone to take away your red Swingline stapler.

SPACING OUT: SPACES AFTER A PERIOD

Unlike the question "How many licks does it take to get to the center of a Tootsie Pop?" the question "How many spaces go after a period at the end of a sentence?" has an answer: On a typewriter, use two. On a computer, use one. Typewriter fonts are called monospaced fonts because every letter, punctuation mark, and space are the same width. Most computer fonts are called proportional fonts because the letters, punctuation marks, and spaces are different widths. An *m* takes up more space than an *i*, for example. With a proportional font, two spaces after a period aren't necessary. The font developers have already taken the space needs into account.

<u>Monospaced, Two Spaces*</u>

```
A 1612 edition of the King James Bible has an
error. Psalm 119 should have read "PRINCES have
persecuted me." Instead it reads "PRINTERS have
persecuted me." Editors and printers find this
funny. A disgruntled typesetter may have done it.
This version is called the "Printers Bible."
```

<u>Proportional, Two Spaces</u>

A 1612 edition of the King James Bible has an error. Psalm 119 should have read "PRINCES have persecuted me." Instead it reads "PRINTERS have persecuted me." Editors and printers find this funny. A disgruntled typesetter may have done it. This version is called the "Printers Bible."

<u>Proportional, One Space</u>

A 1612 edition of the King James Bible has an error. Psalm 119 should have read "PRINCES have persecuted me." Instead it reads "PRINTERS have persecuted me." Editors and printers find this funny. A disgruntled typesetter may have done it. This version is called the "Printers Bible."

*Intentionally written in a choppy style to highlight spaces between sentences.

Twinkle, Twinkle, Little Star: The Asterisk

The word *asterisk* comes from the Latin and Greek words for "little star," and although it's common to hear people call it an "aste-rick" or "aste-rix," the correct pronunciation is "aste-risk."

Asterisk can be a noun or a verb:

An asterisk appears after his name. (noun)

They had to asterisk his name. (verb)

The asterisk goes after something you want to comment on or qualify, and it looks like this: *.

Always remember to include the note you want the asterisk to refer to at the bottom of the page. An asterisk that doesn't point to anything can cause "asterexasperation."

ROFL: *Hysterical* Versus *Hilarious*

When you're ROFL (see page 182, Sunday), describe the joke as hilarious, not hysterical. *Hilarious* means roughly "super funny"; it comes from a Greek word meaning "cheerful." *Hysterical* means "excited." It comes from the same root as *hysteria*, from a Greek word meaning "womb" (coming from the idea—hrumph—that only women were emotionally excitable). Some kinds of laughter can be hysterical. If people are so uncomfortable they laugh in an inappropriate situation like a funeral or while they are being robbed, that is likely hysterical laughter.

That joke was hilarious.

The hostages were hysterical even after being released.

LANGUAGE ROCK STAR: LYNNE TRUSS

Lynne Truss is a British columnist and radio personality who wrote what is one of the best-selling general commentaries on the English language of all time: *Eats, Shoots & Leaves: The Zero Tolerance Approach to Punctuation*, which *Booklist* called an "impassioned manifesto" and *Publishers Weekly* said ranged from "pleasant rant to bemused dismay." The title of the book comes from a joke about a panda that shows how leaving in or taking out a comma from the phrase changes the meaning. The book was originally published in Britain and later published in America where the editors made the unusual decision to stay with the British punctuation rules (when they differed from American rules).

MAKING NAMES THAT END IN *S* OR *Z* PLURAL

You're addressing envelopes, signing a card, or writing an invitation and suddenly you realize you don't know how to make a name that ends in *s* or *z* plural. How do you address a family of people with the last name *Jones* or *Alvarez*?

Add *es* to make names that end in *s* or *z* plural:

The <u>Joneses</u> invite you to dinner.

Season's greetings from the <u>Alvarezes</u>.

Never use an apostrophe to make a name plural! Apostrophes are for possessives.

Quiz: I'll Have the Flounder: *Founder* Versus *Flounder*

If there's no hope, which sentence is correct?

a. I'm worried about Sue; she's floundering in college.

b. I'm worried about Sue; she's foundering in college.

The answer and an explanation are on page 215.

Over the River and Through the Woods: *More Than* Versus *Over*

This one is almost a myth! Although many style books say it is OK to use *more than* and *over* interchangeably, there is a "rule" floating around that you should use *more than* to talk about bigger amounts and *over* to talk about things that are physically above something or in a different location.

Squiggly discovered he had more than one thousand followers.

The company lost more than $36 billion.

Did you see the moon over the skyline tonight?

Come over tonight.

The rule seems to hold most sway in American newsrooms, so if you work in one it's best to play along.

WORD SEARCH: DROPPING PESKY VOWELS: AMERICAN AND BRITISH SPELLING

Part of Noah Webster's maneuver to create an American identity was to simplify and codify American English. In many cases, he did that by dropping "unnecessary" vowels. See if you can find all the words in this list of American and British word pairs.

The answer key is on page 216.

Y	H	L	A	V	E	A	I	D	E	M	G	U	P	D
A	I	M	E	A	N	A	J	T	D	J	X	K	I	A
E	K	W	Y	G	O	L	O	E	H	C	R	A	Q	I
P	E	W	Y	J	I	M	L	E	V	L	F	W	G	D
A	N	K	O	T	W	K	Z	S	D	Y	T	O	Y	E
E	C	M	A	N	E	U	V	E	R	R	K	V	S	A
D	Y	E	S	T	R	O	G	E	N	L	I	B	X	P
I	C	Z	B	G	M	A	N	O	E	U	V	R	E	O
A	L	V	S	U	T	E	O	F	J	G	J	W	Y	L
T	O	C	I	D	E	P	O	H	T	R	O	O	J	C
R	P	D	Y	A	R	C	H	A	E	O	L	O	G	Y
I	E	T	E	S	R	Q	F	E	T	U	S	A	Y	C
C	D	D	B	C	I	R	T	A	I	D	E	P	M	N
J	I	U	O	E	S	T	R	O	G	E	N	J	Q	E
N	A	V	O	R	T	H	O	P	A	E	D	I	C	P
V	G	Y	B	H	T	L	A	V	E	I	D	E	M	X
J	O	A	X	F	U	V	A	I	M	E	K	U	E	L
Z	U	O	E	Q	U	J	L	Q	D	H	H	C	N	W
Z	Z	T	H	P	Q	I	D	N	Y	Q	J	K	L	T
A	N	E	M	I	A	I	M	E	A	K	U	E	L	E

ANEMIA	ENCYCLOPEDIA	FOETUS	MANOEUVRE	ORTHOPEDIC
ANAEMIA	ENCYCLOPAEDIA	LEUKEMIA	MEDIEVAL	ORTHOPAEDIC
ARCHEOLOGY	ESTROGEN	LEUKAEMIA	MEDIAEVAL	PAEDIATRIC
ARCHAEOLOGY	FETUS	MANEUVER	OESTROGEN	PEDIATRIC

MIXED COMPANY: MIXING ASTERISKS WITH OTHER PUNCTUATION

Remember learning about asterisks last week? When you combine an asterisk with other punctuation marks, the asterisk goes after every other mark except the dash.

> **Squiggly won the pie-eating contest by two pies.***
>
> **Outeating last year's champion by two pies,*** **Squiggly won the contest.**
>
> **Squiggly won the pie-eating contest by two pies;*** **he said they were his favorite flavors.**
>
> **Squiggly won by two pies!***
>
> **Squiggly won the pie-eating contest by two pies*** **—and broke a county record.**

*The winning pies were blueberry and gooseberry.

IN A NEW YORK MINUTE: IDIOMS

Idioms are sayings that have become standard English but either aren't grammatically correct or don't take their literal meaning. For example, unnecessary *ofs* should usually be deleted (see page 198, Sunday), but *a couple of* is an accepted idiom, so you correctly write *a couple of feather boas. It's where it's at* is another accepted idiom. If you were talking about a location, you'd leave off the final *at* because doing so doesn't change the meaning (see page 180, Thursday), but you use that expression to explain that something is hip and cool, so you keep the *at*. Idioms that don't go by their literal meaning include *under the weather* (sick) and *raining cats and dogs* (raining hard).

WHO ARE YOU CALLING "THAT"?
WHO VERSUS *THAT*

Unless you want to offend, it's a good idea to use *who* when you're talking about a person and *that* when you're talking about a thing. Using *that* to refer to people makes them seem less than human.

The woman who sat on the hillside laughed loudly.

The rock that sat on the hillside looked ancient.

But here's a problem: what do you do when you're talking about something animate that isn't human, like a pet? It can go either way. I would never refer to my dog as anything less than a *who*, but my fish could probably be a *that*.

You mean my dog who performs wonderful tricks?

You mean my fish that swims upside down?

HOW MANY KENNEDYS SHOWED UP?
MAKING NAMES THAT END IN *Y* PLURAL

Although we typically make words that end in *y* plural by replacing the *y* with *ies*, the same rule does not hold true for family names. For example, it is generally agreed that the plural of *Kennedy* is *Kennedys*.

Have you ever made a pie with blackberries?

I saw two Kennedys on the subway.

Trademarks are usually treated like names. Consider the BlackBerry smartphone. If it were more like a fruit, two of them would be *BlackBerries*. But because it's a brand name, the proper plural is *BlackBerrys*.

Quiz: Let Me _____ Your Interest

Which is correct?

a. Let me pique your interest.

b. Let me peak your interest.

c. Let me peek your interest.

The answer and an explanation are on page 216.

Than Versus Then

A surprising number of people ask me to explain the difference between *than* and *then*.

Then has an element of time. For example, it can mean "next" or "at that time":

We ate, and then we went to the movies.

Movies were a lot cheaper back then.

Than conveys a comparison:

DVDs are more expensive than videocassettes.

Aardvark is taller than Squiggly.

Remember the difference by remembering that *th*a*n* and *comp*a*rison* both have the letter *a* in them, and *th*e*n* and *tim*e both have the letter *e* in them.

Your Head Will Literally Explode

Although *literally* has been used to mean "figuratively" or "virtually" for many years, using it that way drives a lot of people batty. For example, the TV sitcom *How I Met Your Mother* had a character misuse "literally" in a show that highlighted the most annoying thing about each character.

The word *literally* literally means "in a literal sense." Exactly. Without exaggeration. Word for word. It's OK to say California literally had no rain for thirty days (if indeed there had been no rain during that time). It's wrong to say San Diego was literally as dry as the Mojave Desert. (That is unlikely given San Diego's proximity to the ocean.) Unless your co-workers are extremely heinous, you won't literally be thrown to the wolves if you miss your deadline or literally have your head served up on a platter if you don't meet your sales numbers.

When you say your head is going to literally explode, there are a lot of people whose blood pressure literally rises as they imagine putting lit firecrackers in your ears to make

your sentence correct. It's best to avoid using *literally* to add extra emphasis to your writing.

Squiggly's head is about to *literally* explode.

A Question of Drama: The Difference Between a Dash and a Colon

A colon and a dash both introduce a related element after a sentence, but a dash is a more sensational and informal mark than a colon.

The colon usually means you're going to clarify what came before. It coolly informs readers that something more is coming along.

A dash, on the other hand—well, it's quite dramatic. A dashing young man is certainly not an ordinary young man, and if you're dashing off to the store, you're not just going to the store, you're going in a flurry. A dash interrupts the flow of the sentence and tells the reader to get ready for an important or dramatic statement.

Capitalizing Names with Proper Nouns

When something such as a food, a disease, or a product is named after a person or a country (a proper noun), that proper noun is still capitalized. Therefore, you have:

Alzheimer's disease
French fries
French dressing
Spanish rice
Spanish flu
German measles
Japanese noodles
General Tso's chicken
Dutch doors

LANGUAGE ROCK STAR: JAMES MURRAY

James Murray was hired by Britain's Philological Society in 1879 to be the editor of the *Oxford English Dictionary*. Although he wasn't the first editor, he worked on the project for thirty-six years until his death and has become the editor most closely associated with the first edition. He managed the many assistants who worked on the project and built a scriptorium to hold the tons (literally) of paper quotation slips mailed in by thousands of volunteers who scoured publications for the first instances of words and for examples to highlight the different meanings of words.

I'M SO HAPPY THAT I'LL JUMP FOR JOY: SO . . . THAT

Technically, you shouldn't write something like, "I'm so happy." The problem is that *so* is looked down on as an intensifier—a word that modifies *happy* to show that you are happier than just plain old happy. A better sentence would be "I'm very happy," and an even better sentence would use a more extreme word to get the point across: "I'm rapturous."

It's OK to use *so* when you follow it with a *that* (or an implied *that*). Then it is an adverb related to the degree of happiness instead of a vague intensifier.

I was <u>so</u> happy about the sales numbers <u>that</u> I jumped for joy.

Word Scramble: Abstract Nouns

You may have learned that nouns are people, places, and things; but ideas, concepts, and traits can also be nouns. Unscramble some of the abstract nouns listed below.

diceva_____

rayverb_____

gorecua_____

ductnaeio_____

domeref_____

roonh_____

yayllto_____

naip_____

rutts_____

The answer key is on page 216.

Snuck Versus Sneaked

The British are sticking firmly with *sneaked* as the past tense of *sneak*, but Americans have largely accepted *snuck* as an alternative or even preferred form. That's not to say *snuck* is without aggressive, vocal detractors. I regularly receive messages from people who hate it. Unfortunately, linguists and lexicographers say detractors are losing the battle. For example, *American Heritage* notes that *snuck* is increasingly common in newspaper articles and the *Merriam-Webster* calls it standard. Nobody knows where *snuck* came from. Some think it's paralleling *stick/stuck* and *strike/struck*. I only use *snuck* when it fits much better than *sneaked* in the rhythm of a sentence, and I'm prepared for a fight.

Em Dashes Versus En Dashes

You learned the basics of dashes last week on Monday, but (as usual) that's not the end of the story.

There are two different kinds of dashes: the em dash (—) and the en dash (–). Those might seem like strange names, but they make sense when you realize that, traditionally, the em dash was as long as the width of a capital letter M, and the en dash was as long as the width of a capital letter N (meaning an em dash is usually twice as long as an en dash). The em dash was also often the length of the font size. For example, if you were using a 12-point font, the em dash was 12 points long. (Modern font designers don't always follow these rules.) The em dash is what people usually mean when they say "use a dash." The en dash is usually only used to indicate a range of inclusive numbers.

Never use a hyphen in place of a dash. If you can't insert the dash symbol, use two hyphens right next to each other: --.

Whether you are using the longer em dash in a sentence or the shorter en dash to indicate an inclusive range, major style guides recommend no spaces between the dash and the surrounding words.

> **"Squiggly is packing his camping gear—are you coming along?—and then he'll load the car." (The dashes indicate a strong break in the middle of the main sentence. This is most common in dialogue.)**

Most word processing programs can be set to automatically insert the em dash symbol when you type two hyphens without any spaces between words.

OUT OF THE SIDE OF YOUR MOUTH: PARENTHETICAL STATEMENTS

Parenthetical statements are just little asides in your sentences. Depending on how much you want to emphasize these beside-the-fact statements, you can use different punctuation marks to set them off. Commas are the least dramatic, and dashes are the most. Parentheses fall somewhere in the middle.

I'm fantasizing, just fantasizing, about taking a year off to hike the Sierra Rim Trail.

I'm fantasizing (yes, I have a wild imagination) about taking a year off to hike the Sierra Rim Trail.

I'm fantasizing—but don't think I won't do it—about taking a year off to hike the Sierra Rim Trail.

I ONLY EAT CHOCOLATE: MISPLACED MODIFIERS

Misplaced modifiers apply to something you didn't intend to modify. Words like *only* and *almost* are modifiers that are easy to misplace. These sentences mean different things:

I ate <u>only vegetables</u>. (I ate nothing but vegetables— no fruit, no meat, just vegetables.)

I <u>only ate</u> vegetables. (All I did with vegetables was eat them. I didn't plant, harvest, wash, or cook them.)

I failed <u>almost every art class</u>. (I passed a few classes.)

I <u>almost failed</u> every art class. (I got lots of Ds.)

It's easiest to get modifiers right when you put them immediately before the thing they are modifying.

STOP SQUINTING! SQUINTY MODIFIERS

Yesterday you learned about simple misplaced modifiers, but it gets more complicated. In the following sentence, *woman's* is a type of misplaced modifier called a *squinting modifier*:

Squiggly donned a tall <u>woman's</u> hat.

That could mean a tall hat meant to be worn by women, or a hat belonging to a tall woman. If you mean the hat is tall, you can fix the sentence by swapping *tall* so that it comes right before *hat*:

Squiggly donned a woman's tall hat.

But if you mean the woman is tall, you have to rewrite the sentence:

Squiggly donned the hat belonging to the tall woman.

YOUR PARTICIPLE IS DANGLING

Dangling participles sound so risqué! But a participle is just a verb form that ends in *-ing*, and to dangle such a beast simply means to place it in a sentence so that it modifies something unintended. A dangling participle is just a type of misplaced modifier. Here's an example:

Rolling down the hill, Squiggly was frightened that the rocks would crush Aardvark.

Rolling—the participle—refers to Squiggly the way that sentence is written, but it's more likely that the rocks were rolling down the hill. If so, *rolling* is a dangling participle, and the sentence should read as follows:

Rolling down the hill, the rocks frightened Squiggly.

Quiz: You're Asking Me for Advice?

Which is correct?

a. **Squiggly's popular new advisor recommended eating more chocolate.**

b. **Squiggly's popular new adviser recommended eating more chocolate.**

The answer and an explanation are on page 216.

Time Keeps on Ticking: *Because* Versus *Since*

Because and *since* are different, but most people use them interchangeably. In everyday writing, it isn't a crime to misuse these two words. But if you don't want strict grammarians tsking at you, it's easy to figure out the words' formal meanings.

Since deals with time:

Since the incident, people treated her differently.

That example means something happened from the time of the incident. After that time, people treated her differently.

Because deals with something that brings about a result or an effect:

Because the incident was so upsetting, people treated her differently.

Time doesn't enter into that example, so you use *because*.

What?! Interrobang

You're not supposed to mix exclamation points and question marks at the end of a sentence, but aren't you always tempted to when you're writing a surprised question? A question mark alone doesn't get across the shock, outrage, or excitement of the question; but an exclamation point leaves out the whole question part. Many times, people simply give up on the rules and write, "Really?!"

But there's a better way. In 1962, an advertising man named Martin Speckter invented a punctuation mark for people to use at the end of such sentences. He introduced the idea in a magazine he edited called *TYPEtalks* and called for name suggestions. The reader suggestion of *interrobang* (which combined the Latin for "query"—*interrogation*—with *bang*, a printers' term for exclamation point) was eventually accepted as the name for the new mark. (*Exclamaquest* was also considered.) Initially, the mark gained the attention of the media, with Speckter giving print and television interviews, and the *Wall Street Journal* even publishing an editorial praising the development. Although the interrobang never gained widespread use after its initial celebrated debut, there are Unicode and HTML codes for it, and it is included in the Wingdings 2 font.

(LEAVE IT OUT) PARENTHESES AND COMMAS

The best way to understand when to use a comma with parentheses is to determine whether you'd need a comma without the part in parentheses. In the following sentence, if I remove the part in parentheses, the sentence would still need a comma, so I include one:

> I like Java Jungle (the art changes frequently), but the Brickhouse Bakery is quieter.

> I like Java Jungle, but the Brickhouse Bakery is quieter.

In the following example, the pared-down sentence doesn't need a comma, so I don't include one after the parentheses:

> I like Java Jungle (the art changes frequently) and Dreamers.

> I like Java Jungle and Dreamers.

QUIZ: ANYWAY VERSUS ANYWAYS

Which way would you say this?

> a. Anyways, how soon can you reupholster the sofa?
> b. Anyway, how soon can you reupholster the sofa?

The answer and an explanation are on page 216.

LANGUAGE ROCK STAR:
HENRY WATSON FOWLER

Henry Watson Fowler (also known as H. W. Fowler) was an Englishman who was educated at Oxford and wrote some of the most influential early works on British English usage. In 1906 he wrote *The King's English* with his brother Francis George Fowler, in 1911 the two brothers wrote the first *Concise Oxford Dictionary*, and in 1926 (after his brother's death) H. W. Fowler published *Modern English Usage*, which remains in print in updated form today. Fowler also worked on the first edition of the *Shorter Oxford English Dictionary*, a book that also remains in print today in updated editions.

SHE WAS NOT UNCONCERNED:
DOUBLE NEGATIVES

You know the saying *Two wrongs don't make a right*? Remember that and you can easily remember not to have two negatives in your sentence.

Squiggly doesn't never eat squash. (wrong)

Squiggly doesn't eat squash. (right)

It's easy to spot most negatives—*not*, *none*, *never*, *nothing*, and *no*—but a few, such as *hardly* and *barely*, are less obvious.

Squiggly doesn't hardly ever eat squash. (wrong)

Squiggly hardly ever eats squash. (right)

Occasionally, a double negative makes sense. For example, if someone asks "Was she concerned?" a legitimate, slightly sarcastic response could be *Well, she was not unconcerned*.

Quiz: You're Making Me Hungry: *Barbecue* Versus *Bar-b-que* Versus *BBQ*

Which sentence contains the correct spelling of meat cooked over a fire (that's sometimes smothered in yummy sauce)?

a. I'm craving **barbecue.**
b. I'm craving **bar-b-que.**
c. I'm craving **BBQ.**
d. I'm craving **bar-b-q.**

The answer and an explanation are on page 216.

Could Care Less

Do you grind your teeth when you hear people say they "could care less"? I do, too. Unfortunately, when people use that phrase, they usually aren't in the mood for a logic lesson. You and I both know they mean they *couldn't* care less. They don't care at all. They care as little as they possibly could. But by saying they *could* care less, they're actually saying they do care, at least a little. Argggg. Also unfortunately, *could care less* is an accepted idiom that means exactly the opposite of what it says, and it is used about as often as *couldn't care less*. See page 83, Tuesday, for more on idioms. Maybe the first people who used this phrase were being ironic (see page 74, Sunday), but today most people use it without thinking.

WORD SEARCH: BRITISH AND AMERICAN WORDS

Along with the specific changes in American spelling that Noah Webster introduced (page 16, Wednesday), other changes are simply the result of language changing more over time in the United States than in Britain. For example, British English has been more likely to retain irregular past tense forms of verbs. See if you can find all the words in this list of American and British past tense word pairs. (The American spelling in each pair is listed above the British spelling.)

The answer key is on page 217.

M	G	Q	K	V	F	R	A	M	E	D	L	X
R	E	C	S	P	I	L	L	E	D	I	V	Y
D	H	L	E	A	R	N	E	D	N	Y	I	C
A	E	W	K	H	J	L	R	T	L	I	P	S
D	G	L	U	S	X	E	Q	L	D	U	N	N
N	E	B	I	T	L	I	O	P	S	H	X	D
J	Q	L	J	O	B	U	R	N	E	D	R	O
S	F	P	L	Z	P	N	Y	C	W	E	G	N
T	W	O	G	E	D	S	P	Y	A	Q	M	R
S	A	D	E	Y	P	H	J	M	H	Q	E	P
H	Z	F	R	X	L	S	E	D	O	W	C	K
J	O	R	B	E	E	D	O	R	K	P	D	E
P	T	S	Y	U	A	T	E	Q	C	T	K	L
G	T	P	N	J	R	M	X	P	V	P	G	U
D	Z	E	E	Q	N	N	T	O	A	A	S	D
J	C	L	F	L	T	O	T	N	P	E	B	Q
E	H	T	M	J	R	R	Q	E	M	L	L	F

BURNED	DREAMT	LEAPED	SPELT	SPOILED
BURNT	LEARNED	LEAPT	SPILLED	SPOILT
DREAMED	LEARNT	SPELLED	SPILT	

A Common Error: Comma Splice

Commas are tricky because there are so many different ways you can use them, but one of the most common uses is to separate two main clauses that are connected by a coordinating conjunction:

Squiggly cowered under a rock, and Aardvark threw sticks. (right)

Squiggly cowered under a rock is a complete sentence, and *Aardvark threw sticks* is also a complete sentence. To join them with a comma, you need the word *and* or some other coordinating conjunction. If you just put a comma between them, that's an error called a "comma splice."

Squiggly cowered under a rock, Aardvark threw sticks. (wrong)

The Rent Is Due: *Because of* Versus *Due to*

The rule is that *because of* modifies verbs, and *due to* modifies nouns (usually following a linking verb such as *was* or *appears*). If you're having trouble figuring out which phrase you need, *because of* is almost always the better choice.

I'm late because of the storm.

Because of the storm, I'm driving cautiously.

It's better to reserve *due to* for times when you mean something other than *on account of* such as *owed* or *expected*. For example, "Pay the money that is due to her," or "She was due to arrive yesterday."

PHAT! IT'S THE BOMB: WRITING WITH SLANG

Like regionalisms, slang can give your characters life and personality when you're writing fiction; but unlike regionalisms, slang can change quickly and make your work sound dated. People in the South have said *y'all* for at least a hundred years, but kids probably won't be saying *fo' shizzle* in ten years. You can use slang to create a setting from the past—*squaresville* will place your story in the 1950s and *groovy* will place your story in the 1960s—but you don't want to lose authenticity by using slang from the wrong era or carelessly using current slang in your writing in a way that will make it dated in the future.

A WHOLE NOTHER TOPIC

From the e-mail I receive, I'd say *a-whole-nother* bothers a "whole lotta" people. Maybe if they knew how it compares to other words and phrases that are similar, they wouldn't hate it so much. *A-whole-nother* is one of only a few nonprofane examples in English of tmesis (occasionally also called infixing). You probably know that a prefix goes at the beginning of a word, and a suffix goes at the end. Well, with tmesis a word goes in the middle of another word. *A-whole-nother* is usually considered tmesis instead of infixing because the thing splitting *another* is a whole word instead of a suffix- or prefix-like element. Other examples of tmesis include:

abso-bloomin'-lutely

any-old-how

Quiz: *A Lot* Versus *Alot* Versus *Allot*

Which of the following is incorrect?

   a. Fluffy liked hiking a lot.
   b. Squiggly found alot of bugs scary.
   c. Aardvark decided to allot each camper two books
   of matches.

The answer and an explanation are on page 217.

Who's on First: *First* Versus *Firstly*

Although it's acceptable to order sentences firstly, secondly, thirdly, etc., in your writing, many people (including me) prefer first, second, and third for their simplicity and directness. *Firstly* just sounds fussy to me. And for heaven's sake, don't mix the two forms. If you start with *first*, *second* is next, not *secondly*. I have been known to disagree with *Strunk and White*, but in this case I like their take on the matter: "Do not dress words up by adding 'ly' to them, as though putting a hat on a horse."

A Mighty Stretch: *May* Versus *Might*

May and *might* both indicate that something is possible, but something that may happen is more likely than something that might happen. You may go to a party if George Clooney invites you, but you might go to a party if creepy George from next door invites you. Use *might* when something is a mighty stretch. For example, bungee jumping terrifies me, so if someone asked me to go on a corporate bungee-jumping trip, it's unlikely I would go. I could be convinced if I thought my job depended on it, but it would be a mighty stretch, and not just because of those stretchy cords.

An exception is that *might* is the past tense of *may*, so it would be correct to say "Squiggly might have gone hiking in the foothills last weekend."

Squiggly bungee jumping? It's a mighty stretch of the imagination (and the cord)!

Run Along Now: Run-On Sentences

Many people believe that run-on sentences are just really long sentences, but actually they are sentences that lack punctuation. They can be long or short:

He ran home she stayed behind.

That's a run-on sentence because it's written without any internal punctuation. I've fused together two complete sentences—*He ran home* and *She stayed behind*—which is why run-on sentences are also called fused sentences. Run-ons are easy to fix with periods, semicolons, and commas with coordinating conjunctions.

He ran home. She stayed behind.

He ran home; she stayed behind.

He ran home, and she stayed behind.

It's Not a Dumb Teenager with Zits: Oxymoron

You create an oxymoron by joining two words that don't seem to go together. Common oxymorons are often meant to be funny, but they are also used to point out flaws:

Is there really such a thing as military intelligence, government organization, or an industrial park?

More literary examples come from Shakespeare, for example, Hamlet's oxymoron, "I must be <u>cruel only to be kind</u>," and Juliet's from *Romeo and Juliet*, "Parting is such <u>sweet sorrow</u>."

Language Rock Star: Robert W. Burchfield

Robert W. Burchfield was a New Zealander who studied at Oxford University under J. R. R. Tolkien and C. S. Lewis and became a noted lexicographer. He spent twenty-five years editing the four-volume second edition of the *Oxford English Dictionary* and was the editor in chief of the *OED* from 1971 to 1984. His work was frequently controversial, and he successfully fought to include such things as definitions of racial slurs, words from foreign countries, and trademarks in the *OED*. He ended up in court over some issues and also received death threats. In 1996, he released what was perhaps his most controversial work—an extensive revision of H. W. Fowler's *Modern English Usage*.

And Then . . . : Starting a Sentence with a Coordinating Conjunction

You may have learned that it's wrong to start a sentence with a coordinating conjunction such as *and* or *but*, but it's not wrong—it's just informal. You are creating something like a sentence fragment when you start a sentence with a conjunction, which is why schools teach students not to do it; but sometimes starting a sentence with a conjunction creates a desired effect (dramatic or conversational).

I had never seen that wine before. And I'm a sommelier.

This style choice is often seen in the edited work of respected writers. Because such constructions draw attention to themselves, don't overdo it. You don't want every other sentence in your work jumping around waving its hands in the air.

WORD SCRAMBLE: MODALS

Modals are helping verbs that tell you more about the speaker's attitude toward the main verb, for example, the possibility that something will happen or the necessity of something happening: we *should* go. Unscramble this list of common modals.

doulc_____

himgt_____

stum_____

eden_____

lashl_____

oldwu_____

The answer key is on page 217.

COME ON, BABY, LIGHT MY FIRE: *FLAMMABLE* VERSUS *INFLAMMABLE*

Flammable and *inflammable* both mean "easy to burn." *Inflammable* is the original word, but in the 1920s, according to *Merriam-Webster's Dictionary of English Usage*, the National Fire Protection Association started encouraging people to use *flammable* instead because they worried people could mistakenly think "inflammable" meant "not flammable." Academics were inflamed (get it?) because they didn't appreciate the NFPA promoting "corrupt" words, and linguists have groused about *flammable* ever since.

If safety is important, it's best to use *flammable* or some other phrase like *burns easily*. In other cases, you can use whichever word you like.

I Wish I Were a Rich Girl: The Subjunctive Mood

If I were a space traveler, I could learn the grammar rules of languages on other planets. But I'm not a space traveler, and I never will be, which is why I wrote "If I were" instead of "If I was."

English verbs have moods, and when you're being wishful, hopeful, or fanciful, you write in something called the subjunctive mood. *Were* is a subjunctive verb (the subjunctive form of *to be*), and you use it to write about things that aren't real or true. For example, in *The Wizard of Oz* when the cowardly lion sings, "If I were king of the forest," he is fantasizing about all the things he would do if he were brave. He's not courageous, he's just imagining, so *if I were* is the correct statement. Similarly, in *Fiddler on the Roof* when Tevye sings "If I were a rich man," he is fantasizing about what he would do if he were rich. He's not, he's just imagining, so again, *If I were* is the correct statement.

I were often follows the word *if,* because *if* usually means you are wishing or imagining, and *I were* often comes before wishful words like *would* or *could.*

Conversely, when a situation could be true, then it is right to say *If I was.* This is called the indicative mood. For example, you could say

If I was at the mall on Thursday, I would have seen the sale, so I'm pretty sure I was there on Friday.

If I was rude, I will make it up to you.

LET'S NOT FIGHT: SERIAL COMMAS

Many people call it "the comma before the *and*," but its formal name is the serial comma, Oxford comma, or Harvard comma. Whether to use it as I do here in the phrase *red, white, and blue*, is a matter of great contention, but it doesn't need to be. Many people were taught they must always use the serial comma, and many other people were taught that it's an abomination, but the truth is that it's a style choice. I'm a fan of the serial comma, but newspapers and magazines often leave it out to save space (when doing so doesn't cause confusion). Books and other formal works usually favor its use.

HOW MUCH MORE? *THAN I* VERSUS *THAN ME*

Does Squiggly like chocolate more than I or more than me? This is a huge grammar controversy.

Than is a preposition, and only object pronouns (e.g., *me*) follow prepositions, making the correct choice *Squiggly likes chocolate more than me*. However, such a sentence could also mean *Squiggly likes chocolate more than [he likes] me*.

Some people believe *than* can also be a conjunction, which would make *I* an acceptable choice and lead to sentences with implied endings:

Squiggly likes chocolate more than I [do].

Squiggly likes chocolate more than I [like chocolate].

There's no right answer. I recommend adding the implied words to avoid ambiguity (and a battle).

AYE, AYE, CAPTION: WRITING CAPTIONS

People often wonder how to write photo captions: *Bobby McGee and Me* or *Bobby McGee and I*?

It's awkward to apply grammar rules to such captions because they aren't sentences, they're sentence fragments. First, you must decipher the implied meaning. Are you trying to say "This is a photo of Bobby McGee and *me*," or "This is Bobby McGee and *I* in Baton Rouge"?

Because in the second example it's also acceptable in most cases to write "This is Bobby McGee and *me* in Baton Rogue," the better choice is to caption your photos "Bobby McGee and me." Finally! A case where the lyrics are (mostly) right. (Check out page 203, Tuesday, for more on *I* and *me*.)

LET'S TAKE UP A COLLECTION: COLLECTIVE NOUNS

Collective nouns generally describe collections of people: the band, the orchestra, the faculty, the family, etc. There are no hard-and-fast rules here, only trends. Americans tend to treat collective nouns as singular and the British tend to treat them as plural, so in America you'd be more likely to hear *The team is here* and in Britain you'd be more likely to hear *The team are here*. Whether you're emphasizing the individual members or the collective group also influences whether you use a singular or plural verb: *The team [members] are swapping jerseys* or *The team is going to Boston*.

IN SPITE OF THE RULES: IN SPITE OF VERSUS DESPITE

Choose the best sentence:

a) She ran well despite having old shoes.

b) She ran well in spite of having old shoes.

c) She ran well in despite of having old shoes.

The answer and an explanation are on page 217.

I HOPE THE JUDGE ISN'T UNINTERESTED: UNINTERESTED VERSUS DISINTERESTED

An uninterested person is bored, unconcerned, or indifferent; a disinterested person is impartial, unbiased, or has no stake in the outcome. If you're on trial, you want a disinterested judge. Unless you're a lawyer, the word you're generally looking for is *uninterested*, but a quick news search shows that *disinterested* is frequently misused by the media. Here's how to use them properly:

Squiggly couldn't help yawning; he was uninterested in fishing stories.

The ex-wife can hardly be considered a disinterested party.

Interestingly, *disinterested* and *uninterested* had the opposite meanings long ago, and at some point in the eighteenth century the meanings were swapped to what they are today.

Quiz: Tents and Porpoises: On Purpose

Which saying is correct?

 a. For all intensive purposes.
 b. For all intents and purposes.
 c. For all tents and porpoises.

The answer and an explanation are on page 217.

Introducing, Commas! Commas with Introductory Elements

Sometimes introductory elements require a comma and sometimes it's up to you. If you have a modifying or conditional phrase, dependent clause, or conjunctive adverb at the beginning, you need a comma after it:

As a potter, I'm always on the lookout for good clay.

If you ran, you would win.

Meanwhile, chaos broke out across the land.

If you have a short prepositional phrase, you get to decide whether a comma is necessary for the flow of the sentence.

In the beginning, there was a snail.

After the show we went for dinner.

Language Rock Star: George Orwell

George Orwell, born Eric Arthur Blair in India but raised in Britain, was a prolific nonfiction writer during his time, but today he is best known for his novels *Animal Farm* and *Nineteen Eighty-four*. *Nineteen Eighty-four* insightfully highlights how language can be used to guide or control thoughts. For example, Orwell invented a language for the novel called Newspeak in which undesirable or negative words are removed or replaced—*bad* becomes *ungood*, for example—with the idea that over time if people can't think negative thoughts, they won't be able to dissent. The novel also introduced the terms *Big Brother*, *thought police*, and *doublethink*.

There's a Name for That? Anadiplosis

In the last tip, I ended one sentence and started the next with the same words: "Nineteen Eighty-four." There's actually a name for that; it's call anadiplosis, which comes from the Greek for "doubling back." Although my writing wasn't particularly beautiful, when used eloquently, anadiplosis can be an effective literary tool for leading readers or listeners through a series of related ideas:

> **Fear leads to <u>anger</u>. <u>Anger</u> leads to <u>hate</u>. <u>Hate</u> leads to suffering. (Yoda, in *Star Wars*)**

> **Suffering breeds <u>character</u>; <u>character</u> breeds <u>faith</u>; in the end <u>faith</u> will not disappoint. (Jesse Jackson at the 1988 Democratic National Convention)**

The Data Dilemma: Is *Data* Singular or Plural?

The question seems easy enough: Is *data* singular or plural? Unfortunately, the answer is both. The singular noun *datum*, meaning "a given fact or assumption," and its plural, *data,* came to English from Latin long ago; but in the late nineteenth century *data* also took on the meaning "facts and figures," and when that happened, people started treating it as singular. Which path you take comes down to style and personal preference. Many academic and scientific fields, as well as many publishers and newspapers, still treat *data* as plural, as in *The data are compelling*; but in everyday writing it is more commonly treated as singular, as in *The data is compelling*.

IT'S A MEDIA CONSPIRACY: IS *MEDIA* SINGULAR OR PLURAL?

Yesterday I told you that *data*, originally plural, has taken on an acceptable English singular status, but what of *media*, a similarly Latin-based word? Traditionally, *medium* is singular and *media* is plural. Television is (among other things) a medium for communication; when many stations cover one story in excess, you could properly say the media have (note the plural verb) gone wild. Yet, *the media* also can be a collective noun like *the orchestra*. Collective nouns are usually singular in the United States, and it's becoming more common to hear *media* treated as singular. Stick with plural *media* for now, but don't be surprised when it becomes acceptably singular in the future.

MORE ON LATIN PLURALS: NEW ENGLISH PLURAL FORMS

If you have a problem with *media* and *data* being plural, you'll probably also cringe at the Anglicization that sometimes happens to Latin plurals that make their way into English. For example, occasionally you will hear *mediums* used as the plural of *medium*, instead of *media*. More commonly, in most cases, *appendix* and *index* become *appendixes* and *indexes* instead of *appendices* and *indices*, and, even more commonly, *formula* becomes *formulas* instead of *formulae*. The reverse also happens where the plural form ends up being commonly used as singular. For example, *agenda* is the Latin plural of *agendum*, but if you ask your co-workers what the agendum is for your afternoon meeting, you're likely to get strange looks.

Word Search: English Words That Came from Latin

As you've been reading this week, many English words came straight from Latin. Find a sampling of them in the puzzle below!

The answer key is on page 218.

G	H	H	A	G	X	G	A	D	N	E	G	A
P	X	S	C	S	A	P	P	E	N	D	I	X
W	O	M	T	U	W	R	T	G	K	S	S	U
Z	R	E	Q	P	C	A	R	A	D	I	U	S
S	E	M	E	M	A	I	D	E	M	X	T	N
R	A	O	W	A	X	W	Z	W	N	A	A	L
W	K	R	L	C	R	N	N	B	G	V	I	L
N	T	A	I	N	M	U	L	A	X	B	H	L
I	G	N	A	L	U	M	R	O	F	E	G	O
N	V	D	E	T	M	O	L	N	V	A	U	C
D	L	U	V	L	U	Q	H	A	I	C	E	U
E	L	M	Q	G	O	M	O	Q	R	M	O	S
X	V	C	O	A	U	V	A	D	U	V	C	U
F	Q	A	T	A	D	R	E	I	S	O	A	W
O	R	O	J	Z	G	B	Q	L	Z	W	B	X
C	I	P	T	B	I	F	Y	R	Q	M	W	G

AGENDA	CAMPUS	INDEX	MEMORANDUM
ALUMNI	DATA	LARVA	RADIUS
APPENDIX	FORMULA	LOCUS	VIRUS
AXIS	HIATUS	MEDIA	

I, Mignon, Like Writing

My brother David can start a fire without matches, but my husband, Patrick, notes that a lighter is still faster. Why does *Patrick* get commas, but not *David*? Because I have three brothers but only one husband. *David* and *Patrick* are both appositives—words that rename a nearby noun—but *Patrick* is nonrestrictive and *David* is restrictive. In other words, *Patrick* is just an aside to tell you my husband's name, but *David* is important because it tells you which of my brothers has unusual skills. Commas (or parentheses or dashes) are used to set off nonrestrictive elements, but restrictive elements fall in line in the sentence without extra punctuation.

Alumna Are People, Too

Alumni refers to men who have graduated from a school; it is the plural of *alumnus*. A female graduate is an *alumna* and a group of them are *alumnae*. If the homecoming stands are filled with male and female graduates, however, *alumni* is the right choice. As you may have guessed, the words come straight from Latin and cause much confusion (or at least are commonly misused).

Alumnus means "foster son," "pupil," or "to nourish" in Latin. The Latin term for a former school is *alma mater*, meaning "nourishing mother"; therefore, an alumnus can be seen as the foster son (pupil) of the nourishing mother (the school).

Lips Like Sugar: *Like* Versus *Such As*

Like introduces examples that are similar to what you are talking about, and *such as* introduces examples that are exactly what you are talking about.

She paints punctuation marks <u>such as</u> dashes.

If you write a sentence <u>like</u> "Ahoy, throw me a line," you need a comma after the initial interjection.

The first sentence uses *such as* because dashes are among the punctuation marks the artist uses. The second sentence uses *like* because it is unlikely the reader will be writing a sentence with the exact words as the example.

When a Preposition Isn't: Phrasal Verbs

Verbs made up of more than one word are called phrasal verbs. Sometimes it makes sense to end a sentence with the preposition part of the phrasal verb.

He looked like he was going to <u>throw up</u>.

When a phrasal verb is transitive (it does its action to something or someone), you can often split the two parts of the verb, but you usually can't when the verb is intransitive (it doesn't act on anything):

The crook <u>held up</u> the bank.

The crook <u>held</u> the bank <u>up</u>. (The phrasal verb is split, but the sentence still makes sense.)

He <u>dropped out</u> of school.

He <u>dropped</u> school <u>out</u> of. (You can't split this phrasal verb and still make sense.)

Quiz: *Currant Versus Current*

Which two are correct?

   a. Is the current running through the wires?
   b. I like currents in my muffins.
   c. The currant in the river is strong today.
   d. Who would put currants in pie?

The answer and an explanation are on page 218.

What Are You Implying? *Infer Versus Imply*

Speakers *imply* and listeners or readers *infer*. To imply something is to hint at it, to suggest it, whereas to infer is to deduce something that was left unsaid.

   Squiggly, what are you implying?

   "Well, where is the chocolate?" asked Aardvark with a knowing look that implied he already knew the answer.

   Seeing the chocolate fingerprints on Squiggly's tent door, Aardvark inferred what had happened.

   I infer from your demeanor that you aren't going to confess.

Fanboys: Coordinating Conjunctions

Coordinating conjunctions are the little words you use to join other parts of speech:

F—For

A—And

N—Nor

B—But

O—Or

Y—Yet

S—So (*So* can also be a subordinating conjunction.)

The first letter of each word spells the acronym FANBOYS, which can help you remember the whole set. They can join subjects (Squiggly and Aardvark), modifiers (hot or cold), and sentences (Squiggly ran, but Aardvark soldiered on bravely).

Always an Exception: The Contrast Comma

It's OK to use a comma when it wouldn't normally be needed if you want to point out a stark contrast. For example, you don't normally use a comma in sentences like these because there isn't a subject after the conjunction:

Squiggly hid and cowered in fear.

Aardvark was great at catching fish and liked to brag.

However, you can use a comma in such sentences when you want to highlight the contrast between the two parts of the sentence:

Squiggly carefully hid, but carelessly left the campfire burning.

Aardvark was great at catching fish, but hated to touch them.

Once in a Blue Moon: Clichés

Phrases are like furniture: they start out new and wonderful, but over time they become tired and worn. Today's clichés are yesterday's best phrases, metaphors, and similes; that's why they've been overused. But it's time for them to go. Often clichés come from old sayings that don't even make sense to modern readers if they stop to think. Why would you touch something with a ten-foot pole in the first place? Does anyone throw out the bathwater anymore? Come up with a new and wonderful metaphor or simile of your own. If you're lucky, it will be so brilliant it will become the next generation's cliché.

LANGUAGE ROCK STAR: JOHANNES GUTENBERG

Johannes Gutenberg invented the European printing press and is the namesake of the Gutenberg Bible, one of the first books to be printed in mass production using movable type. Although "mass production" in this sense means a little more than one hundred copies, Gutenberg's printing made the Bible more affordable than the handwritten copies available at the time, which could take more than a year to produce, and Gutenberg's printing process was revolutionary and heralded in the age of printed books and the Renaissance. The Gutenberg Bible is the most famous book published by Gutenberg, but it's believed he printed other books earlier, possibly Latin grammar schoolbooks.

A SINGULAR GRAMMAR CONTROVERSY: *THEY* AS A SINGULAR PRONOUN

English doesn't have a good singular pronoun to use when you don't know the sex of the person you're talking about.

Please ask the next guest to remove [his? her? his or her? their?] shoes.

In speech, people already commonly use the plural pronoun *their* in such cases, but many writers object to using *their* as a singular pronoun in writing (and some people even cringe when they hear it in speech). If you wish to be cautious, use *he or she* or *his or her*. If you choose to be bold and use *their*, you'll probably get some flack, but multiple credible style guides will back you up.

WORD SCRAMBLE: SEEK AND DESTROY

Clichés have their place in dialogue but, other than that, it's best to avoid them. See if you can unscramble these common clichés.

igb shif ni a lamls donp_____

cityrious dellik het act_____

eadd sa a odorainl_____

aveh a cine yad_____

eikl het galpue_____

apes ni a dop_____

pelts eilk a glo_____

butronbs sa a lume_____

lods ilek thesocka_____

The answer key is on page 218.

NO ROOM AT THE INN: *INTO* VERSUS *IN TO*

In indicates position. *Into* indicates movement or action. *To* is often part of infinitive verbs and *in* is often part of phrasal verbs, therefore, *in* and *to* sometimes just end up next to each other.

Examples will help!

He broke <u>into</u> a sweat. (*Into* is a preposition and part of the action; it is one word.)

We <u>broke in</u> to the room. (*Broke in* is a phrasal verb. The word *in* belongs with *broke*, not *to*.)

Squiggly walked <u>into</u> the lamppost. (*Into* is a preposition and part of the action.)

Squiggly walked in <u>to hear</u> Aardvark gossiping. (*To hear* is an infinitive verb. *To* belongs with *hear*, not *in*.)

LATIN SCHMATIN: *I.E.* VERSUS *E.G.*

I.e and *e.g.* are both abbreviations for Latin terms. People often use them interchangeably, but they mean different things.

E.g. stands for *exempli gratia*, which means "for example," so you use it to introduce an example:

I like card games, e.g., rummy and crazy eights.

Because I used *e.g.*, you know that I have provided a list of examples of card games I like. It's not a finite list of all card games I like; it's just a few examples. Remember that *e.g.* is for examples because they both start with the letter *e*.

I.e. stands for i*d est* and means roughly "that is" or "in other words," so you use it to introduce a further clarification:

I like to play cards, i.e., rummy and crazy eights.

Because I used *i.e.*, which introduces a clarification, you know that these are the only card games I enjoy. Remember that *i.e.* means roughly "in other words" and they both start with the letter *i*.

Even though these are abbreviations for foreign terms, they have become such a common part of English that you don't need to italicize them. You do, however, need to use periods after each letter. Although it's not a universal rule, it's common to put a comma after the abbreviations.

Finally, don't be intimidated by these abbreviations, or even feel required to use them—they are just abbreviations for the phrases *for example* or *in other words*. You can use the abbreviations wherever you would use those words, and you can write out the words instead of using the abbreviations if you wish.

NAMESAKES

If someone is referred to as "the third," you can use the Roman numeral (*III*) or the Arabic numeral (*3rd*), with no comma after the name. When speaking, we say *the third*, but when writing, don't include the word *the* before the numeral.

Thurston Howell III

Thurston Howell 3rd

Older styles required a comma on both sides of *Jr.* or *Sr.,* but most modern guides leave it out, just as with *III* or *3rd*.

John Kennedy Jr.

Martin Luther King Sr.

Make such designators possessive by simply adding an apostrophe and *s* to the end:

John Kennedy Jr.'s death was a tragedy.

I love Thurston Howell III's yacht.

HAVE SOME REGARD: *IRREGARDLESS*

Before you insist that *irregardless* is not a word, take a moment to ponder the meaning of the word *word*. It's a unit of language people use to convey a meaning.

Although it is true that the origin of *irregardless* is corrupt (most likely a combination of *irrespective* and *regardless*), when people say it (and many do), I know what they are trying to convey, and so do you.

Rest assured that although *irregardless* is in many dictionaries, it is still labeled as "nonstandard." It is a word, but it isn't a word you should use.

I'm Every Woman: Woman Versus Female

Thankfully, sex differences rarely come up these days when talking about professions; a male nurse or a female doctor isn't extraordinary, for example. Nevertheless, when someone becomes the first man or woman to do something, we still talk about it. Although some people object to using *female* as an adjective because to them it sounds scientific (we studied eight hundred female frogs) and because in some cultures it is used in a negative or objectifying way as a noun (bring on the females!), *female*, not *woman*, is the traditional adjective and makes the most sense when you draw parallels to *male* and *man*: Nancy Pelosi was the first female Speaker of the House.

Neither . . . Nor, Either . . . Or

You can't have a *neither* without a *nor*. The universe won't stand for it! *Neither* means "not either," which by definition means two choices.

Neither Squiggly nor Aardvark went to the store.

He gave me neither love nor security.

It wouldn't make sense to write these sentences:

Squiggly nor Aardvark went to the store.

He gave me neither love and security.

Either matches up with *or* just as *neither* matches up with *nor* when you're discussing two items in the same sentence.

You can have either chocolate or celery, but not both.

He went to either the school or the store.

Quiz: *Oral* Versus *Verbal*

Which of these arguments could have been made on paper?

a. They presented oral arguments.
b. They had a verbal agreement.

The answer and an explanation are on page 218.

Where's My Latte? Compound Words

While looking up how to write *coffeehouse*, I encountered two common problems: different dictionaries handle compound words differently and formatting can change over time.

It appears that it used to be hyphenated (*coffee-house*), but now it's most commonly written as a closed compound (*coffeehouse*). At least one dictionary entry also shows the open compound (*coffee house*) as an acceptable alternative.

I decided to go with *coffeehouse*. If you're not sure whether a word is an open compound, closed compound, or hyphenated compound, the only thing you can do is pick a dictionary and go with its recommendation. In fact, whenever you're unsure of any word, a dictionary is the best place to start.

I'M SO TENSE I CAN'T THINK: VERB TENSES

If you grew up speaking English, you probably use the right verb tense naturally, but can't really explain what the tenses imply. Here's a handy chart.

PRESENT	Example Sentence	Meaning of Sentence
Simple present	Jack walks.	It is a fact that Jack walks.
Present progressive	Jack is walking.	Jack is in the act of walking now with no end to the walk.
Present perfect	Jack has walked.	Jack finished his walk at some time in the past.*
PAST		
Simple past	Jack walked.	Jack walked at some point in the past.
Past progressive	Jack was walking.	In the past, Jack was walking, but we don't know when he stopped or if he did.
Past perfect	Jack had walked.	In the past, Jack walked and then the walk ended.
FUTURE		
Simple future	Jack will walk.	In the future, Jack will get out of the house and walk.
Future progressive	Jack will be walking.	Jack will walk in the future. And walk and walk. Who knows when it will end.
Future perfect	Jack will have walked.	In the future, Jack will have walked (again!) and then gone home and put his feet up.

*Yes, it's weird that you use the *present* perfect to talk about something that happened in the past.

IF YOU WANT TO WRITE BETTER: CONDITIONAL SENTENCES AND COMMAS

Sentences with "if clauses" are called conditional sentences. The action depends on something else.

When the "if clause" is at the beginning of the sentence, you need a comma. When the "if clause" is at the end of the sentence, you don't. (Note that in some instances, you can substitute the word *when* for *if*.)

If you have questions, let me know.

If I hadn't gotten up so early, I wouldn't be tired.

Let me know if you have questions.

I wouldn't be tired if I hadn't gotten up so early.

A COMPLIMENTARY TIP: *COMPLEMENT* VERSUS *COMPLIMENT*

A *compliment* (with an *i*) is a word of praise, and something *complimentary* is something given without charge. To remember that these words use an *i*, remember the following nice sentences about yourself. (Put the emphasis on the *I* when you read it.)

I like to give compliments.

I like to give complimentary treats to the guests.

Then, by default, the other kind of *complement* (with an *e*) means something that pairs well with something else or is a complete amount. You can remember that *complete* and *complement* both have *e*'s.

The eggnog complements the éclairs.

The ship had its full complement of sailors.

Language Rock Star: Shakespeare

Although best known for his plays, William Shakespeare lived in the time of Early Modern English and also had a significant influence on English vocabulary. The origin of thousands of words, such as *courtship*, *dwindle*, *frugal*, and *silliness* are attributed to Shakespeare because they're the first uses cataloged by the *Oxford English Dictionary*. *OED* volunteers were more likely to scour Shakespeare's works for quotations than to peruse obscure works, but even if he wasn't the true originator of the words attributed to him, he still certainly played a part in popularizing them and recording them for future generations.

So Many Men, So Little Time: The Plural of *Mister*

The plural of *Mister* (*Mr.*) is *Messieurs* (*Messrs.*). It is common to use abbreviations when writing a letter, so if you are writing to multiple men, this is the correct way to format your salutation:

Dear Messrs. Smith, Chen, and Wright,

The plural of *Mistress* (*Mrs.*) is *Mmes.* (short for *Mesdames*), and the plural of *Miss* is *Misses*. The plural of *Ms.*, which originated in the 1950s, is less clear. Various sources report that the plural of *Ms.* can be *Mses.*, *Mss.*, or *Mmes.*

In American English, a period is required after the abbreviations; in British English, no punctuation is required after the abbreviations.

QUIZ: *HOME IN* VERSUS *HONE IN*

How did you come to that answer?

a. I was able to home in on the answer.

b. I was able to hone in on the answer.

The answer and an explanation are on page 218.

MOTHER, MAY I: *CAN* VERSUS *MAY*

Traditionally, *can* refers to what is possible and *may* refers to what is permissible.

Can you run faster than Joe?

May I accompany you to the dance?

So when students ask if they *can* go to the bathroom, they're asking teachers to speculate on a very personal matter.

In modern practice, however, people tend to use *can* and *may* interchangeably and major style guides say it's acceptable in informal situations (such as a classroom conversation). Still, if you're in a formal situation such as an interview or speaking to people in tuxedos for any reason, it's polite to use *may* when asking permission.

WORD SEARCH: GREEK'S INFLUENCE ON ENGLISH

Greek had a significant influence on English. Not only do many English words come directly from Greek, but many Latin words that entered the English language themselves came from Greek. The plural of some Greek words have been Anglicized; for example, the traditional plurals of *octopus* and *trauma* would be *octopodes* and *traumata*, but of course we commonly say *octopuses* and *traumas*. See if you can find all of the words below, which came to English directly from Greek.

The answer key is on page 219.

W	J	O	Q	C	A	I	R	E	T	I	R	C
V	Y	S	Q	K	I	N	E	T	I	C	T	A
K	A	P	B	J	J	M	P	F	L	A	S	U
A	J	M	A	A	T	Y	A	A	C	C	I	N
L	J	W	F	M	F	H	T	X	A	T	N	X
E	R	A	F	U	R	P	H	A	T	U	O	U
I	Z	I	J	A	E	A	O	I	A	S	G	X
D	O	G	V	R	W	R	S	O	S	J	A	X
O	C	L	J	T	F	G	E	N	T	G	T	N
S	T	A	D	V	A	I	K	A	R	K	O	G
C	O	T	Q	I	F	L	C	R	O	U	R	V
O	P	S	A	D	R	L	T	A	P	D	P	C
P	U	O	X	U	C	A	O	P	H	O	O	N
E	S	N	K	S	A	C	S	Y	E	S	R	M
G	J	Q	B	Y	S	A	T	S	C	E	T	A
L	G	P	G	Y	P	O	R	T	N	E	S	L
D	V	A	H	L	K	Y	Q	L	P	D	Z	R

CACTUS	ECSTASY	KINETIC	PARANOIA
CALLIGRAPHY	ENTROPY	KUDOS	PATHOS
CATASTROPHE	GAIA	NOSTALGIA	PROTAGONIST
CRITERIA	KALEIDOSCOPE	OCTOPUS	TRAUMA

Watch Those Commas!

Commas may seem incidental, but putting them in the wrong place can change your meaning. In 2006, for example, two Canadian firms went to court over what came to be called "the million-dollar comma" because the point under dispute hinged on the interpretation of how one comma was placed in the contract. The "rule" that you put in a comma when you'd pause while speaking isn't a real rule. It's more like a guideline: it's a decent way to guess if you don't have a clue, but if the accuracy of what you're writing actually matters, you need to learn the real rules.

O'Clock in a Title

O'clock is a contraction for *of the clock*—it's one word—so when you write a title caps headline, you'd expect to use a lowercase *c* just as you would in the last half of any other contraction (*O'clock*), right?

Well, even though that format makes sense and it's recommended by *The Chicago Manual of Style*, most news outlets capitalize the *c* (*O'Clock*).

Up until the mid-1900s some major publications wrote it as *o'Clock*, presumably because the *o* stands for *of*, which isn't capitalized in headlines.

There isn't a definitive rule about how to handle *o'clock* in headlines. Today, *O'Clock* is the most common form, *O'clock* is defensible, and *o'Clock* is archaic.

TYPO TROUBLE, TAKE TWO

It could be conceded that British TV personality Eamonn Holmes has a difficult name to spell, but marketers and copy editors are held to a pretty high standard when they work on a game called *Spell*. So when the game's publisher, DDS Media, discovered that they had spelled the host's name wrong (*Eamon*, leaving off the second *n*) on the cover of their interactive *Spell* DVD, they were forced to reprint ten thousand copies. Ouch! A quick and dirty tip for proofreading is to always have multiple people proof your work. Every set of eyes increases the chance of finding an error like that one.

AS A GRAMMAR MAVEN, I . . . : STARTING A SENTENCE WITH A MODIFYING PHRASE

As a grammar writer, I often settle bets. One bet I settle is whether it's OK to start a sentence with a phrase such as *as a grammar writer*. It's right the way I did it in the first sentence, but there are ways to mess it up:

As a grammar writer, my writing is often scrutinized. (wrong)

As a grammar writer, people often ask me questions. (wrong)

Those examples are wrong because the part that directly follows the *as-a-grammar-writer* part must be the grammar writer. The person who writes about grammar is me, not my writing and not people, as is written in the incorrect sentences. You must immediately follow that introductory element with the thing or person it's describing.

Quiz: *Nauseous* Versus *Nauseated*

Which of the following would make a grammar stickler vomit?

a. Ugh, I feel nauseous.
b. That smell made me nauseated.
c. What is that nauseating smell?

The answer and an explanation are on page 219.

Take Your Preventive Medicine: *Preventive* Versus *Preventative*

Often when there are two nearly identical words that mean the same thing, such as *preventive* and *preventative*, everyone presumes that one of them is wrong—usually the longer one. Such logic would suggest that *preventative* is a bad word, and some of the experts I respect the most say it is. But it's not. It pains me to say it, but *preventive* and *preventative* mean the same thing and are interchangeable. *Preventative* has been around as an adjective and a noun for over three hundred years. You may certainly choose to use the sleeker *preventive*, but don't chide people who prefer the longer form.

A Tough Breakup: Splitting Infinitives

My idea of fun is splitting infinitives. To understand my thrill, you have to know that some people believe it's wrong to split them. An infinitive is just a fancy name for a type of verb with the word *to* in front of it, for example, *to leave*.

Blame Latin for the logic behind the nineteenth-century rule about not splitting infinitives. In Latin there are no two-word infinitives, so it's impossible to split one, and English teachers decided that if it couldn't be done in Latin, it shouldn't be done in English.

But notions change over time, and today almost everyone agrees that it's OK to split infinitives, especially when you'd have to change the meaning of the sentence to avoid the split. English isn't Latin, after all.

Here's an example of a sentence with a split infinitive:

Squiggly decided <u>to</u> quickly <u>leave</u>.

Quickly splits the infinitive *to leave*: to <u>quickly</u> leave.

If you try to unsplit the verb, you can actually change the meaning. For example, you might say

Squiggly decided quickly <u>to leave</u>.

Now, instead of saying Squiggly quickly left, you're saying Squiggly quickly *made the decision* to leave.

Squiggly decided to quickly leave.

Squiggly decided quickly to leave.

COMMAS BETWEEN TWO ADJECTIVES

When you're trying to decide whether to put a comma between two adjectives, ask yourself these two questions:

1. **Can you put the word *and* between the adjectives and still have a sentence that makes sense?**
2. **Can you reverse the order of the adjectives and still have a sentence that makes sense?**

If you answer yes to both those questions, you have coordinate adjectives and you use a comma between them. You can use *and* between the adjectives and reverse the order in the following sentences, so you use a comma.

Squiggly is a yellow and tubby snail.

Squiggly is a tubby and yellow snail.

Squiggly is a tubby, yellow snail.

IT'S A FREE COUNTRY: FOR FREE

Many readers object to the phrase *for free*, but many language commentators say it's so commonly used that it's standard English. *For* leads the reader to expect an amount (e.g., for $5), but the concept of free correlates to "free of charge," which isn't an amount, so *for free of charge* doesn't make much sense. Your sentence will almost always mean the same thing if you leave out the word *for*, and if not, you can usually rewrite it. Rewriting isn't absolutely necessary, but it's a good idea.

Would you like to get into the concert for free?

Would you like to get into the concert free?

Language Rock Stars: The Simplified Spelling Societies

The U.K. Spelling Society and the American Literacy Council are two long-standing groups that support spelling reform as a way to speed learning and improve English literacy. Many prominent citizens have supported simplified spelling in the past, most notably Benjamin Franklin (developed his own simplified alphabet), Andrew Carnegie (funded the American Simplified Spelling Board), and Theodore Roosevelt (signed an executive order requiring reformed spelling in government documents but rescinded it after receiving significant negative feedback). Noah Webster was the most successful proponent of simplified spelling, introducing many reformed spellings into his dictionary.

In the Beginning: *However*

Although you may have heard otherwise, it's fine to start a sentence with *however*. You just need to know when to use a comma because *however* can mean two different things, and if you don't get the comma right, you risk confusing your readers.

If you use *however* at the beginning of a sentence without a comma, *however* means "in whatever manner" or "to whatever extent."

However hard Squiggly tried, he couldn't make Aardvark laugh.

If you use *however* at the beginning of a sentence with a comma, *however* means "nevertheless."

However, Squiggly's jokes weren't very funny.

Word Scramble: Free Gifts Are an Unexpected Surprise: Redundant Phrases

See if you can unjumble the annoyingly wordy or redundant phrases below.

og eahad nda_____

fierb ommnet_____

ned ultres_____

ijon hetregot_____

laque valhes_____

uret tafc_____

pinot ni meit_____

The answer key is on page 219.

My Website Is on the Internet

Is the Internet one specific place or is it a collection of things? Most language experts believe the Internet is one specific entity, which would make *Internet* a proper noun that should be capitalized. The same is true of *Web* because it refers to one specific thing: the World Wide Web. On the other hand, the Web is populated by many different websites, making *website* a common noun that isn't capitalized. This is a style choice, though. If you choose the open compound, *Web* in *Web site* is capitalized, and a few people disagree and use *Website* or *internet*.

JUST SEND ME A MESSAGE: *E-MAIL* OR *EMAIL*?

Office-based red-pen wars have been started over whether the word *e-mail* should be hyphenated. *E-mail* is short for *electronic mail*. In the beginning, almost everyone hyphenated it because it made sense: people argued that *electronic* (and its abbreviation *e*) modified *mail*, not *message*, and you'd use a hyphen to show that.

Send me an electronic-mail message.

But people who considered themselves cutting edge started dropping the hyphen. It was simpler, shorter, more stylish. Traditionalists called these people lazy and uninformed.

You could argue that compound nouns lose their hyphens over time (*cry-baby* recently became *crybaby* in the *Shorter Oxford English Dictionary*, for example) but *e-mail* isn't a compound noun, it is a compound modifier.

Most modern style guides still recommend the hyphen (*The Chicago Manual of Style* and *The AP Stylebook*, for example), but e-mail systems used by millions of people don't use the hyphen (Google and Yahoo!, for example). Although I prefer *e-mail*, I believe it's a losing battle. Current trends are away from hyphens.

Another peeve of traditionalists is the use of *e-mail* as a noun. They hate it when you say "Send me an e-mail," because you are sending a message, and *e-mail* just denotes the type of message. You should say "Send me an e-mail message." The same argument applies to *text message*.

Again, I see the logic, but think it's a losing battle. Still, if you want to play it safe, send e-mail messages and text messages, not emails and texts.

COMMA TUTU: COMMAS WITH *TOO*

Whether you use a comma with *too* at the end of a sentence (or in the middle) depends on how much emphasis you want to place on the word.

I won the Nobel Prize too.

I won the Nobel Prize, too.

It's a subtle difference, but in the above sentence pair, there's more of a pause when you use a comma, which places more emphasis on the word *too*. You can hear it if you imagine someone saying the first sentence with excitement upon realizing he or she has bumped into a fellow prize winner, and then imagine someone snobbishly saying the second sentence to emphasize the Nobel Prize is just one of his or her many laurels.

LOG ME ON COACH, I'M READY TO PLAY

Log in, *log on*, *log out*, and *log off* are all considered to be phrasal verbs. In other words, they are two-word verbs. *Log in* and *log on* both refer to entering the necessary information to access some kind of computer system or network, and the words are interchangeable, as are *log out* and *log off*. In certain cases, the two parts of the word can be split:

She logged Grammar Girl off the system.

If you use the words as adjectives (for example, before a noun), use a hyphen:

Who puts flashing graphics on log-in pages anymore?

(See entry on page 155, Monday, for more on using hyphens with adjectives when they come before nouns.)

The Funnest Grammar Tip Ever

Fun is a word in flux. I like to think of it as a *fun* continuum. On one end you have *fun*, the noun, and everyone is happy to cluster around and be associated with it.

We had fun. (good)

If you move on to *fun*, the adjective, you've got a smaller but still significant group of people who will give their approval.

Squiggly throws a fun party. (acceptable)

And then, as you move on down the continuum, you've got a very small group of people who are willing to grab *funner* and *funnest* by the shoulders and give them a big welcoming hug.

That was the funnest party I've ever attended. (not recommended)

Whose Leg Are You Talking About? Whose for Inanimate Objects

Has it ever struck you as weird that you have to use *whose* to refer to something inanimate, such as a table leg? Since *who* refers to people, shouldn't the possessive form—*whose*—also refer only to people? It's one of those quirks of the English language that we don't have a possessive pronoun for inanimate objects, so we're stuck with *whose* in such cases. No need to fret about it.

That is the table whose leg is broken.

It's not necessary, but if such sentences bother you, you can almost always rephrase them.

That is the table with a broken leg.

Quiz: Rest Assured: *Assure* Versus *Ensure* Versus *Insure*

Assure, *ensure*, and *insure* sound a lot alike but mean different things. Choose the correct sentence:

a. I assure you the apples are appealing.

b. I ensure you the apples are appealing.

c. I insure you the apples are appealing.

The answer and an explanation are on page 219.

Take Me Home: *Bring* Versus *Take*

Whether you use *bring* or *take* depends on your point of reference for the action. People bring things to the place you are, and they take things somewhere else.

Bring me a soda.

Take out the garbage.

The choice gets trickier when you start considering the future. If you're talking at the mall, for example, it would be correct to say, "You should take Sheila to the dance on Friday." But if you're speaking in a way that imagines everyone is already at the dance, it's OK to say something like, "We'll be at the dance on Friday. You should bring Sheila."

Bubbles and Lines: The Origins of the Sentence Diagram

Sentence diagramming got its start in 1847 when S. W. Clark, principal of the East Bloomfield Academy, published *A Practical Grammar*, which contained balloon diagrams—the predecessor to today's line diagrams.

There were a few competing diagramming systems in the 1800s and eventually a line diagram system created by Alonzo Reed and Brainerd Kellogg, professors at the Brooklyn Polytechnic Institute, published in *Graded Lessons in English* (1875) and *Higher Lessons in English* (1877), won out. The method, which was taught extensively up to the 1970s, is known after the inventors as the Reed-Kellogg system.

In the Reed-Kellogg system, nouns, verbs, and direct objects are placed on a horizontal line and separated by short vertical lines. Adjectives, adverbs, and prepositional phrases are placed on horizontal lines extending below the main horizontal line.

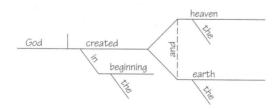

Making Acronyms Plural

By far the most common way to make an acronym plural is to simply add an *s* to the end: *CDs*.

There are a few holdouts who insist on using an *apostrophe s* (*CD's*), but they are in the minority and lost a big supporter when the *New York Times* recently changed its style and dropped the apostrophe from such cases.

Note that you even add an *s* to make an acronym plural if it's not the final word that would be pluralized if you wrote out the words. For example, the plural of *run batted in* is <u>runs</u> *batted in*, but the *s* goes on the end, not on the *r*: *RBIs*.

Janus Words

Alert: Roman gods are fiddling with our language! Actually, they're not, but a word that has two opposing meanings is called a Janus word, named after the two-faced Roman god, Janus. For example, *sanction* is a Janus word because it can mean "to approve" or "to condemn," "a reward" or "a punishment."

The protest was actually a state-sanctioned event.

Imposing sanctions on countries has had mixed results.

Other Janus words include *cleave* ("to cling to" or "to separate"), *screen* ("to review, show" or "to display, hide, or shield from view"), and *trim* ("to remove things" or "to add things").

THERE'S A NAME FOR THAT? EGGCORNS

The name *eggcorn* comes from a 2003 discussion on the Language Log website about a woman who misheard the word *acorn* as *eggcorn*. Such a change isn't a mondegreen because it doesn't create a new meaning, and it isn't a spoonerism (or a malapropism) because the swapped words sound the same—they're homophones.

Other examples of eggcorns include *coming down the pipe* instead of *coming down the pike* and *chomping at the bit* instead of *champing at the bit*. Many of the most common eggcorns seem to insert homophones in familiar phrases, such as H-E-R-E for H-E-A-R in *here, here* and T-O-W instead of T-O-E in *toe the line*.

ANOTHER PAINFUL BREAKUP: SPLITTING VERBS

Grammar pops up in the strangest places, such as the hiccup between Chief Justice John Roberts and Barack Obama during the presidential inauguration. The oath of office reads, "I <u>will</u> faithfully <u>execute</u> the office . . ." Because the adverb *faithfully* splits the verb phrase *will execute*, the construction is called a split verb. Although splitting verbs isn't wrong, Roberts tends to avoid it his writings, and when he got flustered after Obama jumped in too soon, he stated the oath without the split verb: "<u>will</u> <u>execute</u> the office faithfully." The meaning doesn't change, but the men repeated the oath in private so nobody could claim that Obama wasn't properly sworn in.

Quiz: Tiddledywinks: The Tilde

Circle the entries that show a proper use of the tilde in formal writing.

a. It's an El Niño year.
b. It is ~10 miles to the store.
c. We had 8~12 eggs left in the fridge.

The answer and an explanation are on page 219.

That Is Sound Advice: *Advice* Versus *Advise*

The basic difference between *advice* and *advise* is that *advice* is a noun and *advise* is a verb—the act of giving advice.

Aardvark advised Squiggly to stop dreaming of the carnival and get a job.

The advice was not well received.

Advice is one of those nouns, like *courage*, that aren't something solid you can see, but *advice* ends in *ice*, and it's easy to remember that a block of ice is a noun. (Even though the *ice* in *advice* has nothing to do with frozen water, thinking of it that way can help you remember which word to use.)

Word Search: *I* Before *E*, Except After *C* (and Except When It Doesn't Work)

Students often learn the spelling rule "i before *e*, except after *c*," but it's not a very good rule; there are many exceptions. When completing this puzzle, try to memorize the correct spelling for these exceptions.

The answer key is on page 220.

X	N	F	O	L	J	D	N	E	M	L	G
Y	E	S	M	W	H	H	N	R	E	I	L
N	I	U	Y	O	B	I	E	U	W	H	A
T	T	R	G	S	E	Y	P	S	E	C	C
N	H	G	F	F	B	T	O	I	I	S	I
E	E	I	F	M	Z	S	C	E	R	O	E
I	R	A	X	L	U	I	S	L	D	C	R
C	C	L	V	T	N	E	O	H	E	I	O
I	G	N	I	E	B	F	D	C	C	E	E
F	S	O	V	E	R	E	I	G	N	T	Y
F	T	P	V	E	Z	I	E	S	E	Y	X
U	N	O	E	W	U	R	L	M	I	I	K
S	E	V	E	C	N	X	A	A	C	L	S
Q	I	N	Z	K	I	N	K	L	S	M	S
I	C	F	H	M	E	E	E	I	M	N	E
C	N	C	O	L	V	Q	S	T	D	N	Y
D	A	V	N	E	I	G	H	B	O	R	P

ANCIENT	SPECIES	FEISTY	NEITHER	WEIRD
GLACIER	SUFFICIENT	KALEIDOSCOPE	SEIZE	
SCIENCE	BEING	LEISURE	SOVEREIGNTY	
SOCIETY	CAFFEINE	NEIGHBOR	VEIN	

THE BIGGER THEY ARE, THE HARDER THEY FALL: CONJUNCTIVE ADVERBS AND SEMICOLONS

When joining two sentences with a conjunctive adverb—a word like *however*, *indeed*, or *meanwhile*—use a semicolon instead of a comma. Conjunctive adverbs tend to be longer than conjunctions, and semicolons are "bigger" than commas, so you can remember that big words joining sentences need a "big" punctuation mark: the semicolon.

Aardvark built a fire; meanwhile, Squiggly wandered around the forest.

Squiggly found some tinder; however, Aardvark had already built the fire.

You could also use a period in each of these sentences in place of the semicolon, but a comma would be wrong.

SHE DISCREETLY CORRECTED HIS GRAMMAR: *DISCREET* VERSUS *DISCRETE*

Discreet means "tactful" or "cautious," and *discrete* means "separate," "distinct," or "unconnected." A quick news search will demonstrate how shockingly often these two words are confused. Don't be one of the writers or editors who makes this error! The quick and dirty tip is to remember that *discrete* ends with a spelling like the Greek island Crete, which is also separate, distinct, and unconnected.

She discreetly gave her sorority sister the secret handshake.

There were two discrete choices.

Lock Them Up: *Pled* Versus *Pleaded*

Although *pled* and *pleaded* are both in common use, language sticklers prefer *have pleaded*, and professional writers seem to have gotten the message: a Google News search returns about sixty-two times as many hits for *pleaded guilty* as for *pled guilty*.

Here are some of the more interesting examples from news stories (with emphasis added):

> **"The owners of a small South Carolina company *have pleaded* guilty to charging the Pentagon nearly $1 million for shipping two 19-cent washers to Texas."
> —The Blog of Legal Times**

> **"A Michigan mail carrier accused of stashing thousands of pieces of mail in a storage unit instead of delivering them *has pleaded* guilty to deserting her route."—Associated Press**

Spell It Out: Redundant Acronyms

Be careful when using acronyms and initialisms—remember, they stand for something! It's easy to forget and utter a redundancy, such as "PIN number." Since *PIN* stands for *personal identification number*, it's redundant to put the word *number* after *PIN*. Here are some other common stumbling blocks:

> **ATM machine (*ATM* stands for *automatic teller machine*.)**

> **PC computer (*PC* stands for *personal computer*.)**

If your audience won't know what the abbreviation stands for and you feel you need the redundancy for clarity, don't use the abbreviation, spell out the words.

Quiz: Capitalization

Which of the following is incorrect?

a. He suffers from depression.

b. He lived through the great depression.

The answer and an explanation are on page 220.

Whoever Versus Whomever

Like *who* and *whom*, the choice between their friends *whoever* and *whomever* depends on identifying the subject and object position. Use *whoever* or *whomever* (instead of *who* or *whom*) when the word relates to two clauses:

Give the doughnuts to <u>him. He</u> arrives first.

Give the doughnuts to <u>whoever</u> arrives first.

I'll give the doughnuts to <u>him</u>. You chose <u>him</u>.

I'll give the doughnuts to <u>whomever</u> you chose.

If both of the pronouns in the two implied sentences are in the object case (could hypothetically be *him*), use *whomever*. It's the same trick you learned for *who* and *whom* on page 16, Thursday, but this time it's double: two *hims* equal *whom*.

You've Earned That Title: Title Capitalization

There are at least four ways to format a title. The less common methods include capitalizing every letter, writing the headline as a sentence, and capitalizing every word:

GRAMMAR GIRL WOULD KILL FOR SOME ICED TEA (all caps)

Grammar Girl would kill for some iced tea (sentence style)

Grammar Girl Would Kill For Some Iced Tea (cap all words)

The fourth method is significantly more complex, but also more widely accepted:

Capitalize the first and last word in the title.

Capitalize all nouns, pronouns, verbs, adjectives, and adverbs.

Don't capitalize the conjunctions *and*, *but*, *for*, *or*, and *nor*; the prepositions *as* and *to*; or the articles *a*, *an*, and *the* (unless they are the first or last word of a title).

Don't capitalize prepositions unless they are used adjectivally, adverbially, or as conjunctions, or if they are stressed. (Note: some styles deviate from this point and capitalize any preposition four letters long or longer.)

Grammar Girl Would Kill for Some Iced Tea

Iced Tea Was Hidden beneath the Counter

A Snail Helped Grammar Girl Look Up the Recipe

That Animal Is out of Control

HOW THINGS CHANGE:
COMPOUND WORDS AND HYPHENS

The rules about when to hyphenate a compound word are squidgy because compound words evolve from open compound (two separate words), to hyphenated compound, to closed compound (one word with the two parts shoved together)—and sometimes back again—and the changes can seem arbitrary. For example, the *Shorter Oxford English Dictionary* eliminated sixteen thousand hyphenated words in 2007. Some words (*leap-frog*) advanced to closed compound form (*leapfrog*), and other words (*pot-belly*) reverted back to open compound form (*pot belly*). The best advice is to pick a dictionary and consult it when you aren't sure.

HIS MAJESTY, AARDVARK:
CAPITALIZING HONORIFICS

Those grand-sounding names for nobility or other important people are called *styles of nobility*, *honorific titles*, or *terms of respect*, and most editors (but not those at the Associated Press) consider them to be proper nouns because they are standing in for someone's name. So they are capitalized in the same way that *Mom* or *Dad* are capitalized when you use them directly in place of someone's name.

Michelle Obama hugged Her Majesty.

By doing so, the First Lady caused quite a stir.

One assumes William and Harry hugged the Queen Mother.

Language Rock Star: William Strunk Jr.

William Strunk Jr. was the original author of the iconic usage guide *The Elements of Style*, often referred to today as simply *Strunk and White*, a name that makes reference to E. B. White, who revised the book in later years. Strunk privately published the first edition of the forty-three-page book in 1918 for his English students at Cornell University, who referred to it as "the little book." Since then, the book has sold over 10 million copies in various editions and although it has grown in page count, it is still appealing because of the clear and concise rules laid out by its original author.

Back and Forth: Formatting Dialogue

Let's say you're writing the great American novel. You'll probably have multiple characters who talk to each other. It would look like this:

> **"No," said Squiggly. "I don't want to go."**
>
> **"I don't care. I want you to come," Aardvark insisted.**
>
> **Squiggly pulled his hand out of Aardvark's. "No! No! No!" Squiggly paused before continuing. "You never listen to me!"**

OK, I didn't say that *I* was able to write the great American novel, but at least the formatting is correct because I started a new paragraph every time I changed the speaker.

Word Scramble: Conjunctive Adverbs

A few weeks ago, you learned to use a semicolon to join sentences with conjunctive adverbs. See if you can unscramble some conjunctive adverbs that weren't mentioned in that tip.

wanyya_____

anryietlc_____

nifalyl_____

ehenc_____

nsetaid_____

leiewisk_____

ymneal_____

rteherofe_____

The answer key is on page 220.

Cement Your Relationship:
Concrete versus *Cement*

If you want to maintain your dignity in home improvement stores, it's helpful to remember that cement is the powder you mix with other materials to create solid concrete. But these words also have noninterchangeable, metaphorical meanings apart from patio construction. For example, you can cement a relationship, where *cement* means to bind or join (just like you cement the materials together to make concrete). Similarly, *concrete* means something solid in the sense that it's the opposite of abstract. You can have solid plans for dinner, or concrete plans for dinner.

Come on Everybody, Do the Locomotion: *Everyone* Versus *Everybody*

Do these sentences mean the same thing?

Everybody is doing the brand-new dance now.
Everyone is doing the brand-new dance now.

The answer and an explanation are on page 220.

arnieTen

Before and After: Hyphens

Ah, hyphens. My least favorite punctuation mark. Sometimes the same set of words can take one—or not.

Take the compound modifier *bead trimmed*. If it comes before a noun, you hyphenate *bead-trimmed*, but if it comes after a noun, you don't hyphenate *bead trimmed*.

She loved the bead-trimmed T-shirt.

Her favorite T-shirt was bead trimmed.

The rule is the same whether you're combining two adjectives or an adjective and an adverb (so long as the adverb doesn't end in -*ly*). (See page 167, Monday, for the exceptions.)

The much-loved man didn't know what hit him.

He knew he was much loved.

If Versus *Whether*

In many cases *if* and *whether* are interchangeable, but it's important to use *if* when you have a conditional sentence and *whether* when you mean "regardless of whether."

Here's a pair of examples where *if* and *whether* are not interchangeable:

Call Squiggly if you are going to arrive on Friday.

Call Squiggly whether or not you are going to arrive on Friday.

The first sentence is conditional and means Aardvark is only expected to call if he is coming. The second sentence is not conditional and means Aardvark is expected to call regardless of whether he is coming.

WHETHER VERSUS WHETHER OR NOT

Have you ever wondered whether (or not?) you need to put an *or not* after *whether*?

Often, the *or not* is just extra fluff and should be left off. For example, in this sentence adding an *or not* wouldn't change the meaning or emphasis:

Squiggly didn't know whether Aardvark was coming.

On the other hand, you need the full phrase *whether or not* when you mean "regardless of whether." It shows that there is equal emphasis on both options:

Call Squiggly whether or not you are going to arrive on Friday.

TITLE TIPS: FORMATTING TITLES

The most common way to format titles of newspapers, movies, books, plays, etc., is to put them in italics. In the past, you could choose between underlining and italics (as long as you were consistent—do you get tired of hearing me say that?), but now that website and e-mail addresses are often automatically underlined by computers, italics is the safe way to go.

When you're mentioning shorter works such as poems, articles, chapter titles, and names of songs, use quotation marks.

Yesterday I read the *New York Times*, watched *Casablanca*, and listened to "Life Is a Highway."

Quiz: Making Compound Words Plural

Which of the following are incorrect?

a. I went to see my sisters-in-law.
b. I went to see my sister-in-laws.
c. How many attorneys general are there?
d. How many attorney generals are there?

The answer and an explanation are on page 220.

But I Love Their Style:
Simple Versus *Simplistic*

Designers on HGTV have a bad habit of saying *simplistic* when they mean *simple*; for example, "The modern room was designed to be sleek and simplistic."

That's incorrect if they are trying to say something good about their design.

Simplistic means something is oversimplified or lacking something important. For example, if I were to say that *affect* is a verb and *effect* is a noun, without talking about the exceptions, that would be a simplistic explanation. I left out important details—the exceptions.

Simple indicates their modern room is clean, unadorned, or not overdone. That's clearly what the designers mean when they're talking about their work.

Bad: Linking Verbs Versus Action Verbs

I know that the difference between linking verbs and action verbs sounds like a big semantic "So what?" but it actually matters for some things that people get all worked up about, such as whether to say you "feel bad" or "feel badly" when you are regretful. So bear with me on this one.

Action verbs are exactly what they sound like: they describe actions. Verbs such as *run*, *jump*, and *swim* are action verbs.

Linking verbs, on the other hand, describe a state of being. Linking verbs connect words. Verbs such as *is*, *seem*, *appear*, and *become* are linking verbs.

The complication is that some verbs—the sensing verbs such as *feel* and *smell*—can be both linking verbs and action verbs. To figure out whether you're dealing with a linking verb or an action verb, test whether you can replace the verb with a form of *to be*. If so, then it's probably a linking verb.

He feels bad.

In the above sentence, *feels* is a linking verb because if you replace *feels* with the word *is*, the sentence still makes sense (though, of course, the meaning is changed): He is bad.

See what happens when *feels* is an action verb:

He feels badly.

Replacing *feels* with *is* doesn't work when the verb is active. "He is badly" doesn't make sense.

The reason you say "I feel bad" when you are regretful is that you follow action verbs with adverbs and linking verbs with adjectives (predicate adjectives to be fussy about it). *Bad* is an adjective, and *badly* is an adverb. So the correct statement is "I feel bad."

Hyphens for Clarity, Part I

Sometimes it doesn't matter what the regular rule is, you need a hyphen for clarity. For example, if I wrote the following sentence, it could be interpreted the wrong way.

The silver jewelry cart has cute, affordable stuff.

What do you think I mean? Is the cart silver or does the vendor sell silver jewelry? The way it's written, it means the cart is silver, but what I mean is that it has silver jewelry, so I have to add a hyphen:

The silver-jewelry cart has cute, affordable stuff.

Now it's clear that the jewelry is silver.

Hyperbole

When you exaggerate something to the point of obvious ridiculousness, that is hyperbole:

She gets a gazillion messages every day.

I could eat a whole cow.

I'll die if I have to talk to him again.

Hyperbole can also be a useful literary device for adding emphasis or making a point more vivid:

"[He] fired the shot heard round the world." —from Ralph Waldo Emerson's "Concord Hymn"

"There was no hurry . . . nothing to see outside of Maycomb County." —from Harper Lee's *To Kill a Mockingbird*

Hyperbole is commonly mispronounced. The correct pronunciation is *hye-PER-buh-lee*, not *hyper-bowl*.

Language Rock Star: E. B. White

Elwyn Brooks White made significant literary contributions in a few different areas. The author of the beloved children's books *Charlotte's Web* and *Stuart Little*, he also was an editor at the *New Yorker* for many decades. He was a student of William Strunk Jr. at Cornell and revised *The Elements of Style* after Strunk's death, creating the edition of the book now commonly called *Strunk and White*. White's contributions to the book were significant, nearly doubling the page count with such additions as an introduction and a concluding chapter that makes style recommendations such as "Avoid fancy words," "Do not affect a breezy manner," and "Use orthodox spelling."

Double Trouble, Take One: *The The*

Have you ever stumbled into a sentence where you needed to write a double *the*? It certainly doesn't sound correct to say, "Did you like the *The Curious Case of Benjamin Button* special effects?" It's grammatically correct, but that doesn't mean your English teacher won't circle it with a red pen and write "awk" for awkward. Usually it's easy to rewrite the sentence another way. Another option is that once you write out a full title, it's fine to shorten it in later references. Using that rule, if your problematic sentence comes late in your document, you could write something like this: *Did you like the* Benjamin Button *special effects?*

QUIZ: BECAUSE IT'S THERE:
CREVICE VERSUS *CREVASSE*

Which sentence tells a story about a scary gap?

> **a. While hiking on the glacier, we had to jump over a gaping crevasse.**
> **b. While hiking on the glacier, we had to jump over a gaping crevice.**

The answer and an explanation are on page 220.

BUYING BOOKS FROM THE STATIONER:
STATIONARY VERSUS *STATIONERY*

Stationary means to stand still, and *stationery* is something on which you write a fancy letter.

> **Please remain stationary while you are being scanned.**

> **Your grandmother would love to receive some nice stationery for her birthday.**

The traditional memory trick is to remember that the *e* in *stationery* stands for *envelope*. Today, you could also say the *e* is for *e-mail*. Either way, *stationery* is related to something you send.

The two words come from the same root. In the Middle Ages most things were sold by traveling salesmen; books were one of the few things sold in fixed stores, which were said to be run by stationers.

WORD SEARCH: LINKING VERBS

Last Sunday, you learned about linking verbs. Find the most common words that can be linking verbs or action verbs in the puzzle below. You know they are linking verbs when you can replace them with *is* (or another verb of being) in your sentence.

The answer key is on page 221.

N	B	D	W	Z	D	Y	T	F	M	E	E
B	P	R	Y	O	L	T	E	G	T	Y	I
P	E	A	J	D	R	E	J	S	M	U	O
G	T	T	S	B	L	G	A	V	T	G	W
S	M	E	L	L	F	T	P	W	L	R	F
K	O	M	R	Q	B	N	D	I	O	O	W
Z	D	E	I	L	S	Y	Y	X	R	W	L
R	M	V	T	Y	K	O	W	Z	P	Q	N
B	C	M	K	J	P	P	A	Y	L	R	S
N	T	G	P	R	O	V	E	N	A	N	L
S	Q	U	K	S	O	U	N	D	P	I	O
U	N	J	R	O	V	E	T	E	P	A	C
E	K	W	B	N	O	J	F	J	E	M	D
C	H	B	A	C	O	L	J	X	A	E	U
P	N	U	I	I	A	P	A	S	R	R	N

APPEAR	LOOK	STAY
FEEL	PROVE	TASTE
GET	REMAIN	TURN
GROW	SMELL	
LIE	SOUND	

Hyphens for Clarity, Part II

Occasionally, when context doesn't make things clear, you may need to use a hyphen when you normally wouldn't to avoid confusion between two words that are spelled the same. Consider the following examples:

I need to re-press them. (The hyphen makes it clear you are referring to your jeans and not your memories.)

We need to re-present it. (The hyphen makes it clear you need to deliver something again rather than make a representation of something.)

I'm going to the co-op. (The hyphen makes it clear you're going to the store and not the chicken coop.)

Are You There, God? It's Me, Grammar Girl: Capitalizing Religious Terms

Capitalize *god* when it is the name of one specific god (a proper noun) in any religion. When the word refers to multiple gods or is a description, it is lowercased:

Different religions have different names for the supreme being, including Allah, Yahweh, and God.

Stories about the Greek gods are entertaining.

The god Apollo is often shown playing the lyre.

Religions and specific sacred texts, such as *Christianity*, *Islam*, *Bible*, and *Koran*, are also capitalized.

Whether words such as *godsend* are capitalized often depends on a publication's religious slant. Secular publications often lowercase the words, and religious publications often capitalize them.

Dancing with Myself

Myself is usually what's called a *reflexive pronoun*. That can be hard to remember, but just think about looking into a mirror and seeing your reflection. You'd say, "I see myself in the mirror." You see your reflection, and *myself* is a *reflexive* pronoun. A reflexive pronoun is always the object of a sentence; it can never be the subject. People seem to have the most trouble when mixing *myself* with other nouns or pronouns. Imagine the sentence without the clutter:

Send the memo to Squiggly and myself. (wrong)

Send the memo to me. (right)

Send the memo to Squiggly and me. (right)

It Was Intense: Intensive Pronouns

Myself and its friends *himself, herself, itself, oneself, ourselves, themselves,* and *yourselves* can also add emphasis to a sentence; when they do, they're then called intensive pronouns. For example, if you saw a robber escape, you could say, "I myself saw the fiend go down the alley." Sure, it's a tad dramatic, but it's grammatically correct.

If you usually get takeout and tonight you cooked dinner from scratch, you could proclaim, "I cooked it myself." Again, *myself* just adds emphasis. The meaning of the sentence doesn't change if you take out the word *myself*; it just has a different feeling.

Quiz: Chaos! *Wreaked* Versus *Wrecked* Versus *Wrought*

Which two are incorrect?

a. If the peeves get loose, they will wreak havoc.

b. If the peeves get loose, they will wreck havoc.

c. It happened before and they wreaked their madness everywhere.

d. It happened before and they wrought their madness everywhere.

e. Don't let them get past the wrought-iron fence.

The answer and an explanation are on page 221.

I'm Hanging Up My Spurs: *Hanged* Versus *Hung*

The past tense of the verb *hang* is a tricky one. If you're talking about killing people by dangling them from a rope, use *hanged*; for everything else—curtains, art—use *hung*. Two examples can help you remember.

First, think of " 'Twas the Night before Christmas": "The stockings were hung by the chimney with care." That's right. Stockings, because they're not people, were hung.

Second, there were a lot of hangings in the Wild West, so imagine an old prospector with a Yosemite Sam accent expressing surprise with a common statement from the time: "Well, I'll be hanged!"

Passive-Aggressive Grammar Tips: Active Voice Versus Passive Voice

Many people believe they should avoid the passive voice and only write in the active voice, but fewer people can define those terms.

In the active voice, the subject is doing something.

Squiggly called Aardvark.

Squiggly, the subject, is doing something: he called Aardvark, the object.

In the passive voice, the target of the action is the subject. Instead of saying, "Squiggly called Aardvark," I would say,

Aardvark was called by Squiggly.

Aardvark is now the subject of the sentence, but he isn't doing anything. Rather, he is the recipient of Squiggly's call.

Active sentences are stronger, usually shorter, and more direct than passive sentences.

Passive sentences aren't incorrect, but often they aren't the best way to phrase things. They can be awkward, vague, and wordy.

With the passive voice, it's easy to omit the person who is responsible for the action. In fact, politicians often use passive voice to intentionally obscure who did something: "mistakes were made" and "promises were broken."

On the other hand, if you don't know who did something, sometimes passive voice is the best choice.

The factory was torched.

Passive voice is often used in scientific writing:

The ants were found to have fleas.

Nevertheless, in most cases, it's better to use the active voice.

AN INDIVIDUALLY WRAPPED TIP: HYPHENS AND ADVERBS—THE "-LY" EXCEPTION

Hyphens. Hyphens. I wish the rules were simpler. When you have multiple modifiers before a noun, sometimes you join them with a hyphen and sometimes you don't.

You use a hyphen when joining compound adjectives before a noun:

Squiggly enjoys <u>blue-streaked cheese</u>.

You also join adjectives and adverbs before a noun with a hyphen:

Squiggly likes <u>well-aged cheese</u>.

But, if the adverb ends in "-ly," you don't join them with a hyphen.

Squiggly always carried <u>individually wrapped cheese</u> in his bag.

SHALL WE DANCE? *SHALL* VERSUS *WILL*

Strunk and White recommended using *shall* like this: *A swimmer in distress cries, "I shall drown; no one will save me!"* But no one in America talks that way anymore; *will* has replaced *shall* in all but a few cases: in legal documents and in lofty prose. *Shall* in a legal sense often indicates explicit obligation: *This lease shall commence on January 1.* Writers and orators use *shall* in a much more uplifting sense. "We shall overcome" comes to mind, as does the end of the Gettysburg Address: *. . . that these dead shall not have died in vain.* You'll also encounter *shall* in playful formality: *Shall we dance?*

LANGUAGE ROCK STAR: BRYAN GARNER

If I had to choose one style guide I couldn't live without, it would be *Garner's Modern American Usage* by Bryan Garner. I find it to be the most comprehensive and evenhanded usage guide on the English language; rarely do I have a question that isn't answered in those pages. (Swoon.) Garner is also a lawyer, the editor in chief of *Black's Law Dictionary*, the author of *A Dictionary of Modern Legal Usage* and *The Elements of Legal Style*, the author of the "Grammar and Usage" chapter in *The Chicago Manual of Style*, and the owner of a company that annually conducts hundreds of writing seminars for lawyers.

IF YOU DON'T MIND MY ASKING . . . : *ME* VERSUS *MY*

Many style guides have commented on which pronoun should come before a gerund, and they come to different answers. Today, the possessive form is usually recommended:

> **Do you mind my making a recommendation? (most common)**

> **Do you mind me making a recommendation? (allowed by some)**

The way to remember that the possessive pronoun—*my*, in this case—is usually the better choice is to consider what you're implying. When you ask if someone minds "me making a recommendation," you're asking if they object to you. When you ask if someone minds "my making a recommendation," you're asking if they object to the act of recommending.

WORD SCRAMBLE: PLURALS

Most English nouns are made plural by adding -s or -es to the end, and you've learned about strange Latin and Greek plurals, but a few odd nouns are the same whether they are singular or plural. See if you can unscramble a few below.

arcraitf_____

reed_____

someo_____

lamons_____

epesh_____

The answer key is on page 221.

WELL, WELL, WELL: *GOOD* VERSUS *WELL*

First, the simple stuff—*good* is an adjective and *well* is usually an adverb, so *good* modifies nouns and *well* usually modifies verbs, making these sentences correct:

He swam well.

He got good grades.

Now, for the more complicated stuff—remember the linking verb/action verb tip from page 158, Sunday? "Pure" linking verbs are verbs of being, such as *is* and *am*, and unlike action verbs, you follow linking verbs with adjectives. Note that at the beginning I said *well* is "usually" an adverb. That's because it can be an adjective, too, which means that both of these sentences are correct:

I am good.

I am well.

THE OPRAH QUESTION: COMPOUND POSSESSION

When writing about possession with two subjects, you have to decide whether the two people possess something together or separately.

The rule is if the two subjects share something, you use one apostrophe s following the second subject. So if Squiggly and Aardvark have the same religious beliefs, it is correct to say

Squiggly and Aardvark's beliefs.

They share beliefs, so they can share an apostrophe s.

On the other hand, if Squiggly and Aardvark have different religious beliefs, then you would say

Squiggly's and Aardvark's beliefs.

They don't share beliefs, so they can't share their apostrophe s.

The quick and dirty tip for remembering the rule is to think about vacations and hair dryers. (In my mind, apostrophes are shaped like little hair dryers.) Imagine that two women are going on the same trip: if they are sharing a vacation, they could share a hair dryer on the trip, so then they can share the apostrophe s (Oprah and Gail's vacation); but if they are each going on their own separate adventure, then they each need their own hair dryer, and they each need their own apostrophe s (Oprah's and Gail's vacations). So an apostrophe s is like a hair dryer: you don't need to bring two if you are going to share a hotel room.

When one of the words is a pronoun, you use an apostrophe s and the possessive pronoun whether they share the item or not:

Squiggly's and my tree is thriving.

Squiggly's and my cars are both dirty.

THE SUSPENSE IS KILLING ME: SUSPENSIVE HYPHENS

Believe it or not, you can suspend hyphens. (I don't mean you can hang them by their toes, although sometimes I'd like to!) Start with a simple sentence:

Squiggly ordered the blue-striped scarf.

But then Squiggly decides to go wild and order two scarves with stripes of different colors. Instead of writing out *blue-striped* and *red-striped*, you can use suspended hyphens and write *striped* only once.

Squiggly ordered blue- and red-striped scarves.

Suspensive hyphens are economical—there's no need to name the second part of the compound when you'll get to it in a second. These hyphens say be patient; it will show up soon.

COME TOGETHER, AND BE PLURAL: COMPOUND SUBJECTS

When two subjects in a sentence are joined by *and*—a compound subject like *Squiggly and Aardvark*—your subject is plural because you have multiple things. It doesn't matter whether the subjects are all singular, all plural, or mixed—the verb is always plural.

Sir Fragalot and Aardvark chased the peeves.

Squiggly and the police officers tracked them with GPS.

The police officers and the forest rangers eventually caught the peeves.

Compound Interest:
Compound Sentences

Just as a compound subject results when you join two subjects, a compound sentence results when you join two sentences (or independent clauses, as they are called when they become part of a larger sentence). You can join the independent clauses with any of the FANBOYS (see page 118, Sunday). Combining independent clauses in this way adds variety to your writing and helps you establish relationships between events.

Squiggly was hungry, so Aardvark went fishing.

Aardvark took the car, and Squiggly rode a bike.

Aardvark took the car, so Squiggly rode a bike.

Does or Make Things Singular or Plural?

When you have two subjects separated by *or*, it can be tricky deciding whether to use a singular or plural verb.

If both subjects are singular, use a singular verb.

Squiggly or Aardvark was stealing the chocolate.

If both subjects are plural, use a plural verb.

The peeves or the children were outraged.

If one subject is singular and one is plural, match the verb to the closest subject.

The peeves or Squiggly was guilty. (The singular noun is closer to the verb; use the singular verb *was*.)

Squiggly or the peeves were guilty. (The plural noun is closer to the verb; use the plural verb *were*.)

Quiz: More on Mixed Subjects

Which of the following are correct?

    a. He or I was going to take the blame.

    b. They or we were going to get in trouble.

    c. Neither the peeves nor Squiggly is owning up to the deed.

    d. Neither Squiggly nor the peeves are owning up to the deed.

The answer and an explanation are on page 221.

Blechyuckiness: *Communicate* Versus *Tell*

When you're tempted to use the word *communicate*, ask yourself if you really mean *tell*. *Communicate* has its place, for example, when you're talking about establishing the ability to exchange ideas:

Aardvark hoped someday he would be able to communicate with the peeves.

Satellite phones made it easier for the firefighters to communicate with each other while fighting forest fires.

But there is no need to use *communicate* when you mean *tell*:

Please communicate to your team that we've changed the meeting time. (wrong)

Please tell your team that we've changed the meeting time. (right)

Apostrophe Attack

Different publications come to different conclusions on how to write things like *writers' strike* and *farmers market*, so don't feel bad if you're confused. It's often possible to make a good argument for either form and it depends on the circumstances. For example, sometimes the farmers own a market (farmers' market) and sometimes they just rent stalls (farmers market).

But here's something that is clear: unless there's only one writer, don't write something like *writer's strike*.

A writers' strike

A writer's strike

A WINK AND A NOD: EMOTICONS

Some people love emoticons—those punctuation-fueled smiley faces and frowns—and some people hate them. The word itself is a blend of *emotion* and *icon*, making it a portmanteau word (see page 27, Tuesday). With so many misunderstandings arising from e-mail because it lacks oral and visual communication cues, a strong argument could be made for including a "wink" to show you're kidding or a "smile" to show you mean to be friendly. But some people think emoticons are childish and unprofessional. Only you can gauge your audience. Although there is no firm rule about emoticon placement, I recommend treating an emoticon like an asterisk and putting it after all other punctuation marks except the dash. :-)

THERE'S A NAME FOR THAT? SYNECDOCHE

Synecdoche is a specific type of metaphor in which you use part of something to describe all of it:

calling a credit card *plastic*

calling sailors *hands*

calling hungry people *mouths to feed*

or use all of something to describe part of it:

saying *use your head* when you mean *use your brain* to think

You'll find synecdoche when a poet fixates on a physical characteristic of a subject, such as his or her eyes or lips, and in literature when a character will refer to another character by a nickname that highlights some part of his or her body:

Here comes "The Mouth" again. Can't we shut him up?

The Inkhorn Controversy

English vocabulary expanded significantly during the Renaissance—a time when the language was evolving from Middle English to Modern English—and as a result, an intellectual battle called the "Inkhorn Controversy" broke out in the mid-1500s and lasted for over a century. An inkhorn was literally a horn used to hold writing ink, and during the Renaissance learned men (inkhorn users) were getting carried away with inventing elaborate new words, largely drawing from Latin and Greek in an attempt to sound important. Many inkhorn terms appeared in Samuel Johnson's dictionary (see page 8, Wednesday). Opponents of the trend thought people who used inkhorn terms sounded pedantic and affected. Inkhorn words that survived to modern day include *celebrate*, *describe*, *immaturity*, *encyclopedia*, *exaggerate*, and *necessitate*.

Double Trouble, Take Two: *Is Is*

Since the 1970s it's become more common to hear sentences such as, "The point is is that we are out of chocolate." The problem is that the second *is* is unnecessary because the subject of the sentence is *the point*. Such offending sentences often start with *The problem is* or *The reason is*. Watch out for them. On the other hand, occasionally a "double is" will appear in an acceptable sentence such as this: *The question is, is there a confectioner nearby?* It's easier to see that this is OK if you substitute a different question: *The question is, how can we get more chocolate?*

QUIZ: ALTERNATIVES

Choose the clearest and most elegant sentence.

a. Dr. Amir prescribed an antiviral drug to prevent and/or treat the flu.

b. Dr. Amir prescribed an antiviral drug to prevent or, if necessary, treat the flu.

c. Dr. Amir prescribed an antiviral drug to prevent and treat the flu.

The answer and an explanation are on page 221.

FARTHER THAN YOU'VE EVER GONE BEFORE: *FURTHER* VERSUS *FARTHER*

Farther refers to physical distance and *further* refers to metaphorical, or figurative, distance. It's easy to remember the difference because *farther* has the word *far* in it, and *far* usually means a physical distance.

I can run farther than you.

There will be no further discussion of the matter.

Sometimes it's not so straightforward. If I've read more of a book than you, I could be farther along (in pages) or further along (in the story). When it's ambiguous like that, you can use either word.

WORD SEARCH: FAILED INKHORN TERMS

Remember learning about inkhorn words last week? As interesting as the inkhorn words that made it into Modern English are the words that didn't make it. (I've included the definitions of these nonsurviving inkhorn words with the word search list.)

The answer key is on page 222.

E	P	N	W	E	E	B	E	E	L	K	H
E	V	V	Y	L	T	F	X	L	N	B	Z
M	Y	Q	L	B	A	G	O	B	O	Y	M
E	U	J	F	I	G	U	L	I	I	E	L
F	I	C	E	S	I	L	E	S	T	M	J
L	S	U	D	S	T	G	T	S	A	A	A
D	U	B	E	O	A	S	E	O	I	C	N
T	O	I	P	P	F	U	D	P	D	E	A
E	R	C	X	N	J	P	I	M	A	R	C
M	B	U	E	U	T	P	G	O	L	A	E
U	E	L	X	P	N	E	N	C	G	T	P
L	C	A	G	J	E	D	O	N	I	E	H
E	E	R	Y	U	G	I	T	I	D	O	A
N	L	Y	A	Y	N	T	I	A	A	K	L
T	L	W	U	L	I	A	O	I	X	M	I
T	I	M	N	W	S	T	N	Y	N	P	Z
T	P	E	T	I	M	E	D	T	Z	W	E

ANACEPHALIZE (to recapitulate)
CUBICULARY (of or pertaining to a bedchamber)
DEMIT (to dismiss or send away)
DIGLADIATION (a combat with swords)
DIGNOTION (a distinction or distinguishing mark)
EMACERATE (emaciate; to waste away)
EXOLETE (obsolete or faded)
EXPEDE (to accomplish)

FATIGATE (to fatigue)
ILLECEBROUS (delicate, alluring)
INCOMPOSSIBLE (incapable of coexisting)
INGENT (immense, very great)
SUPPEDITATE (to supply or furnish)
TEMULENT (drunk)
UNPOSSIBLE (impossible)

The Apostrophe Exception: Making Single Letters Plural

It's shocking, but you make single letters plural by putting an apostrophe before the *s*!

Mind your p's and q's.

The apostrophe makes it clear that you're writing about multiple p's and q's. The apostrophe is especially important when you are writing about a's, i's, and u's because without the apostrophe, readers could easily think you are writing the words *as*, *is*, and *us*.

There are multiple theories about the origin of the phrase *Mind your p's and q's*. My favorite is that bartenders used to shout it out during fights to tell people to watch their pints and quarts.

Woof! Capitalizing Dog Breed Names

In general, the rule for animal breeds is to capitalize the part of the name derived from a proper noun and lowercase the part of the name derived from a common noun.

In the following examples, *English* and *Yorkshire* are derived from proper nouns—the names of places—and thus should be capitalized. On the other hand, *mastiff* is derived from the Latin *mansuétus* for "tame or mild," and *terrier* is derived from Old French *chien terrier* for "dog of the earth, land, or ground"—both common nouns, which means those parts should not be capitalized.

English mastiff

Yorkshire terrier

When in doubt, consult a dictionary.

A Good Reason to Skip Meetings: *Biweekly* Versus *Semiweekly*

Is a biweekly meeting two times a week or every two weeks? *Bi-* means "two," and *semi-* means "half." So a biweekly meeting is every two weeks, and a semiweekly meeting is twice a week. Said another way that takes into account the meaning of the prefix *semi-*, a semiweekly meeting is every half week.

You can remember the difference by noting that a bicycle has two wheels and semisweet chocolate is only half sweet. If you're going to have meetings as often as twice a week (semiweekly), then you'd better supply semisweet chocolate to the attendees! Squiggly would.

Something Up with Which I Will Not Put: Ending a Sentence with a Preposition

One of the biggest grammar myths of all time is that it's blasphemy to end a sentence with a preposition. It's certainly wrong to end a sentence with a preposition when you could leave the darn thing off and doing so wouldn't change the meaning. So, of course, it's wrong to ask, "Where is she at?" It means the same thing as "Where is she?" Leave off the *at*. But nobody expects you to ask, "From where are you?" or "On what did you step?" No need for stuffy-sounding contortions. "Where are you from?" and "What did you step on?" are fine.

QUIZ: TYPOS ARE SICK! [*SIC*]

Writers use *[sic]* to show that an error in a document isn't theirs—it was in the document or quotation before they got their hands on it. What does *[sic]* stand for?

a. Spelling incorrect
b. Latin for "thus"
c. Same in copy
d. Spelling intentionally conserved

The answer and an explanation are on page 222.

IT'S ABOUT TIME: DAYLIGHT-SAVING TIME

I hate daylight-saving time, but if we have to do it, then we should write it properly. I recommend "daylight-saving time"—hyphen, singular, lowercase. Just remember that you are saving time, daylight time, to be exact. (At least that's what they want you to think.) *Daylight-saving* is a compound modifier that applies to *time*.

Since we're talking about time, there are at least two acceptable ways to write *a.m.* and *p.m.*: as lowercase letters with periods after them or as small capitals without periods. Either way, there should be a space between the time and the notation that follows:

2:00 PM

2:00 p.m.

THE CIA WENT SCUBA DIVING IN OCT.: ACRONYMS AND INITIALISMS

Any shortened form of a word is an abbreviation, for example, *Oct.* for *October*; but acronyms are special kinds of abbreviations that can be pronounced as words, such as *OPEC* ("oh-peck" for *Organization of Petroleum Exporting Countries*). That makes them a subset of abbreviations. All acronyms are abbreviations, but not all abbreviations are acronyms. Sometimes acronyms become so entrenched in the language that they become accepted as words in their own right. *Scuba* is such an example; it was originally an acronym for *self-contained underwater breathing apparatus*.

Initialisms are another type of abbreviation. They're often confused with acronyms because they're made up of letters, so they look similar, but they can't be pronounced as words. *FBI* and *CIA* are examples of initialisms because they're made up of the first letters of *Federal Bureau of Investigation* and *Central Intelligence Agency*, respectively, but they aren't usually pronounced as words.

So remember:

Abbreviations are any shortened form of a word.

Acronyms are made from the first letter (or letters) of a string of words but are pronounced as if they were words themselves. Examples include *NASA, NIMBY* (not in my backyard), and *scuba*.

Initialisms are made from the first letter (or letters) of a string of words, but can't be pronounced as words themselves. Examples include *FBI, CIA, FYI* (for your information), and *PR* (public relations).

Let's Go on a Date: Punctuating Dates

We're easing into numbers this week.

When writing out a full date, use a comma to separate the two numbers.

March 16, 1967

Cardinal numbers are counting numbers (e.g., one, two, three)—a quick and dirty tip is to remember that they are the numbers on playing cards. Ordinal numbers indicate the order of something (e.g., first, second, third). In dates, only use an ordinal number before the name of the month. When the number comes after the month, the year is implied:

We'll have a party on March 16 [2009].

When the number comes before the month, the word *day* is implied:

We'll have a party on the 16th [day] of March.

I've Got Your Number: Writing Numbers

When you aren't writing equations, the most common rule for writing numbers is to use words for the numbers one through nine and numerals for everything larger, but the "rules" vary wildly between style guides. Some say to use words for the numbers one to one hundred and any number that can be written with two or three words (e.g., *fifty thousand* or *two hundred thousand*), which is my publisher's style and, therefore, what is used in this book. Typically, people who write business or technical documents are more likely to use numerals liberally, whereas people who write less technical documents are more likely to write out the words for numbers.

Typo Trouble, Take Three

Ballot measures are often boring, obtuse, and poorly written. Pity the copy editor or proofreader. Yet typos on ballots can be costly. Consider the error that seems to have arisen in Arizona because someone didn't know how to write dollars and cents. Proposition 203 was supposed to be for an 80-cent-per-pack tax increase on cigarettes. But the ballot showed an *.80 cent/pack* increase. Eighty cents is 0.80 *dollars*, not 0.80 cents. It can be written as $0.80, but you need the dollar sign in front. Writing *.80 cent* is one-hundredth the intended amount. The proposition passed and courts had to decide which tax to impose.

Quiz: Let's Mix It Up

Let's say you're writing about snail development—a technical subject—and you've decided on a style that says you use words for the numbers one through nine and numerals for anything bigger. But then you come across a sentence where you need to write one number under 10 and one bigger number. Oh, the horror! What do you do?

a. The snail moved two inches yesterday and 12 inches today.

b. The snail moved 2 inches yesterday and twelve inches today.

c. The snail moved 2 inches yesterday and 12 inches today.

d. The snail moved two inches yesterday and twelve inches today.

The answer and an explanation are on page 222.

Quiz: Cuddly Numbers

You know the general rule is to use numerals for numbers over nine, but what do you do when you have two big numbers cuddling up to each other?

   a. We raised 52 12-inch snails.
   b. We raised fifty-two 12-inch snails.
   c. We raised 52 twelve-inch snails.
   d. We raised fifty-two twelve-inch snails.

The answer and an explanation are on page 222.

How to Distort Statistics: Percents Versus Raw Numbers

When you're reading medical, political, or financial news it's important to understand that big percentages can mean small overall increases or decreases. For example, an article that reports a 50 percent increase in the rate of a rare disease may be telling you that instead of 1 in 1,000,000 people getting floogety flork disease every year, now 1.5 people in 1,000,000 get the disease every year. A 50 percent increase sounds a lot scarier than an additional 150 or so people in the United States. Percentages aren't always misleading, but it's often worth it to check out the raw numbers, too.

Percent Versus Percentage

Now that you know to be careful with percents, let's get our terminology right. In some cases *percent* and *percentage* can be interchangeable, but the easiest way to choose the right word for the right situation is to use *percent* with a number and *percentage* without a number. For example,

> **Forty percent of the cakes were missing.**
> (*Percent* with a number)

> **What percentage of the cakes were missing?**
> (*Percentage* without a number)

When writing percents in a sentence, it's better to use the numeral and not the word, even if it's a number less than 10.

> **Squiggly wailed when he heard that 5 percent of the chocolate cakes were stolen.**

The only time you'd write out the word is if the number appears at the beginning of the sentence.

> **Five percent of the chocolate cakes were stolen.**

Next you have to decide whether to use the word *percent* or the symbol for percent. If you're writing a technical or scientific document, most sources recommend using the symbol. If you're writing something where numbers are used less frequently, it's more common to write the word *percent*. Ultimately, it's a style issue, so make a decision and stick with it.

> **Squiggly saw that 5% of the cakes were stolen.**

> **Squiggly saw that 5 percent of the cakes were stolen.**

If you're talking about a percent (or any numeral) that's less than one, make sure you put a zero before the decimal point.

> **Squiggly wished they had taken only 0.5 percent of the cakes.**

THE OWNERSHIP OF TIME

People often ask how to write about a length of time or an amount of money. Do you need an apostrophe? If you do, does it go at the end?

Think of the years, days, minutes, or dollars owning the noun. That means the correct way to write such phrases is with an apostrophe. Then the same rules apply as any other possessive: if your word is singular, add an apostrophe *s*; if it's plural, the apostrophe goes at the end:

One year's time

Twenty years' experience

Two weeks' notice

Don't be confused by the 2002 movie *Two Weeks Notice*—they got it wrong.

ZEROING IN ON ZERO AND DEGREES

When writing the temperature, spacing is important: if you're using the word *degree*, put a space between the number and the word (100 degrees). If you're using the degree symbol, place it right after the number, without a space (100°). And remember, it's not correct to write *minus zero degrees*—zero is neither positive nor negative.

While we're on the subject of zero, another name for it is *oh*. Therefore, it's not technically incorrect to use the word *oh* when reading out numbers, such as telephone numbers or addresses, but many people find it annoying. For some reason those people rarely complain about James Bond's moniker, *double oh seven*. Is it his charisma or his gun?

Only the Beginning: Numbers at the Beginning of a Sentence

When a number falls at the beginning of a sentence, most sources recommend writing out the words:

Forty-two people attended.

But if the number is ridiculously long, it's better to rewrite the sentence so the number is in the middle. This is hard to read:

Twelve thousand eight hundred forty-two people attended the parade.

This is better:

The parade was attended by 12,842 people.

The second sentence uses the often discouraged passive voice, but passive voice is better than writing out a humongous number and risking that your readers' brains will be numb by the time they get to the verb.

Event Planning Grammar: First Annual

Although some usage experts think the phrase *first annual* is fine, and I agree with them because it conveys the idea that you *intend* to have the event every year, enough experts disagree that I recommend avoiding the phrase. To play it safe, leave your annual intentions off your first-year announcement. (Although *inaugural* can be used to indicate that an event is the first in a series, it doesn't automatically convey the idea that an event will occur yearly.)

Second annual, *third annual*, and so on are acceptable because on the second and subsequent occurrences the event has then been repeated on a yearly basis.

QUIZ: MILLIONS

What's the best way to write a large number that will appear in a paragraph of text?

a. Thirty-five million
b. 35 million
c. 35,000,000
d. 35,000,000 million

The answer and an explanation are on page 222.

EVERYTHING COUNTS IN LARGE AMOUNTS: AMOUNT VERSUS NUMBER

The difference between *amount* and *number* is like the difference between *less* and *fewer*. Use *amount* to refer to mass nouns (things you can't count, such as water and furniture) and *number* to refer to count nouns (things you can count, such as glasses of water and chairs).

Aardvark had a large number of lures in his tackle box.

Squiggly put a large amount of spaghetti in the pot.

Often sentences that use *amount* or *number* are unnecessarily wordy and could be tightened up by replacing those words.

Aardvark had many lures in his tackle box.

Squiggly put a lot of spaghetti in the pot.

OSASCOMP: The Order of Adjectives

Most native English speakers intuitively put adjectives in the proper order in sentences without giving it much thought. In fact, many of you will probably be surprised to learn that there is a quasi-official proper order. Surprise! (Imagine Squiggly, Aardvark, and Grammar Girl jumping out from behind furniture and throwing confetti.)

Adjectives should go in the following order, with opinion first and purpose last:

Opinion (ridiculous, crazy, beautiful)
Size (big, small)
Age (old, young)
Shape (round, square)
Color (yellow, blue)
Origin (American, British)
Material (polyester, Styrofoam)
Purpose (swimming, as in swimming pool; shooting, as in shooting range)

For example, these sentences are correct:

Squiggly's crazy, big idea stunned the audience. (opinion, size)

Aardvark threw his old, round, wooden ball at Squiggly. (age, shape, material)

Grammar Girl wanted to swim in the beautiful, blue swimming pool. (opinion, color, purpose)

You Can Leave That Out: Ellipses in Quotations

The most common use of an ellipsis is to indicate an omission. If you want to omit something from a quotation, use an ellipsis to show where you've dropped words or sentences. For example, here's a quotation from Charles Dickens: "I cannot help it; reason has nothing to do with it; I love her against reason."

If I were a journalist under a tight word limit, I'd be tempted to shorten it: "I cannot help it . . . I love her against reason." Taking out the middle part doesn't change the meaning of the sentence. Dot-dot-dot and it's gone, which saves seven words. Clearly, literature and journalism are not the same thing.

From Silicon Valley to the Twin Cities: Popular Names of Regions

Popular names of regions are capitalized:

Badger State

Bay Area

Silicon Valley

Most popular names—such as the Sun Belt or the Fertile Crescent—cover large or ill-defined areas and could be considered singular, but occasionally a popular name will be plural. For example, the name Twin Cities refers to two specific cities (Minneapolis and St. Paul, Minnesota) and therefore is plural.

Silicon Valley is in California.

The Twin Cities are having great weather this week.

LANGUAGE ROCK STAR: WILLIAM SAFIRE

Although William Safire is a well-known political columnist, language lovers know him best as the author of the long-running "On Language" column in the *New York Times* and at least ten popular books on the English language including *On Language* (1981), *Take My Word for It* (1987), *Language Maven Strikes Again* (1991), *No Uncertain Terms* (2003), and *How Not to Write* (2005). His books and columns often include comments (and criticisms) from readers. Safire is a dropout of Syracuse University; was a senior speechwriter for President Richard Nixon; has worked in television, radio, and public relations; and serves on the Pulitzer board.

VOICE LESSONS: FIRST, SECOND, AND THIRD PERSON

A first-person story is told by one person who is letting you into his or her mind. Theirs is the only viewpoint you get.

I'm planning a peeve-hunting expedition.

A second-person story directs the voice at you, the reader. Second person is frequently used in nonfiction writing.

If you're planning a peeve-hunting expedition, be sure to pack your red pen.

A third-person story is told by a narrator who can explain things about all the characters in a story—what they're all doing and thinking.

Grammar Girl was planning a peeve-hunting expedition.

Word Scramble: He's From Where?

Much as we may wish it, there aren't firm rules about how to note that someone comes from a certain country, state, or town. For example, someone from Kansas City is a Kansas Citian, but someone from Jersey City is a Jersey Cityite. Check with each locality to see how it refers to its residents. See if you can unscramble the denizen names below.

gelAnnoi_____

tinsuAtie_____

stainBoon_____

noosHtuain_____

niMnpealitnao_____

coneniiaPh_____

The answer key is on page 223.

A Historic Herb:
A Versus An—Pronunciation

Remember from page 65, Saturday, that *a* goes before words starting with a consonant sound and *an* before words starting with a vowel sound. Since it's the sound that triggers the choice, pronunciation differences can raise hackles. Take the words *historic* and *herb*. Most people pronounce the *h* in *historic*, meaning you'd write *a historic*, but in the eastern U.S. some people drop the *h* and say "istoric." They usually prefer *an historic* because, to them, *historic* starts with a vowel sound. The same problem arises with *herb*, pronounced "erb" in the United States and "herb" in Britain. Go with the choice that fits the most common pronunciation in your region.

WORD SEARCH: COMMON CAPITALIZATIONS

This puzzle will introduce you to twelve more types of words or phrases that are always capitalized. Each underlined word appears separately in the puzzle.

The answer key is on page 223.

B	K	Z	T	T	V	X	X	F	N	O	I	M
Y	M	J	A	Z	Z	A	G	E	Z	A	S	E
F	V	K	K	Z	E	D	O	W	N	T	G	D
F	W	L	C	A	Z	O	R	P	M	R	B	I
K	A	E	B	E	X	M	L	L	T	A	G	C
S	N	E	U	G	A	H	E	H	T	C	N	A
E	I	N	G	X	X	G	B	P	R	A	X	R
G	S	E	R	Z	C	M	M	O	A	N	C	E
A	U	X	M	W	P	A	Q	F	W	G	A	V
E	P	L	N	O	E	F	M	E	L	A	P	H
L	E	S	S	Y	D	O	C	A	I	M	B	Y
D	R	Y	K	R	X	E	L	S	V	A	O	A
D	B	Y	A	X	U	Q	E	T	I	D	Q	P
I	O	D	E	Z	N	P	Y	E	C	P	G	Z
M	W	T	C	A	T	O	I	R	T	A	P	W
I	L	R	E	W	O	T	S	R	A	E	S	C
C	G	H	C	P	E	X	J	P	N	L	Z	S

CIVIL WAR (wars)	(trademarked	(governmental	PROZAC	SUPER BOWL
EASTER	terms)	programs)	(medication	(sporting events)
(holidays)	MAGNA CARTA	MIDDLE AGES	brand names)	THE HAGUE
JAZZ AGE	(historical	(ages)	SEARS TOWER	("The" is part of
(historical periods)	documents)	PATRIOT ACT	(building	the official name
KLEENEX	MEDICARE	(laws)	names)	of this city.)

ELLIPSIS DOTS

Last week you learned how to use an ellipsis; now you just need to know how to make them. An ellipsis consists of exactly three dots called ellipsis points—never two dots, never four dots—just three dots.

Most style guides call for a space between the dots. Type period-space-period-space-period. Just make sure your ellipsis doesn't get broken up and spread out over two lines. If you want to get fancy, most fonts have an ellipsis character you can insert, and that looks even better than mixing periods and dots. Finally, always put a space on each side of the ellipsis.

Hello . . . Is anyone there?

OVERCOME YOUR PAST: *PRIOR TO* VERSUS *BEFORE*

Prior's primary use is as an adjective.

Earnings were $1.1 million for the quarter compared to $3.0 million in the prior year.

I'm sorry; I have a prior engagement.

Prior to is an acceptable idiom, but when you are tempted to use it, in the interest of simplicity, ask yourself if *before* would work just as well.

Prior to becoming an award-winning clown, Bob was an accountant. (acceptable)

Before becoming an award-winning clown, Bob was an accountant. (better)

Squiggly left the party prior to the raid. (acceptable)

Squiggly left the party before the raid. (better)

Think Different: Set Your Expectations for Advertising

A few years ago Apple released an advertising campaign with the slogan *Think Different*, and grammar fiends the world over freaked out (or at least cringed). The problem? *Different* is an adjective, which means it modifies nouns (e.g., *Choose a different color*). Because *think* is a verb, it should be modified by an adverb such as *differently*. To be grammatically correct, the slogan should have been *Think Differently*. It's fine to be outraged, and pat yourself on the back for noticing, but if you expect advertisements to be grammatically correct, you're living in a fantasy world. Think of such campaigns as providing teachable moments.

There's Doughnuts in the Kitchen: *There Is* Versus *There Are*

You've almost certainly uttered something like *There's doughnuts in the kitchen*. I know I have. It rolls off the tongue like a warm French cruller, but it's wrong. *There's* is a contraction for *there is*, and when you write out the words, it jumps out like a crazed kangaroo that you've got a singular verb and a plural subject. *There is doughnuts*. Oh, the horror! It's harder to say, but form the words *there are doughnuts*. Actually, a sentence is usually better anyway if you rewrite it without a dull opener such as *there is* or *there are*. Try something like *Warm doughnuts are waiting in the kitchen*.

Quiz: Out of Fashion

If you want a sundae like they made in the good old days, how do you write the note?

a. Please give me an old fashion sundae.

b. Please give me an old-fashion sundae.

c. Please give me an old-fashioned sundae.

The answer and an explanation are on page 223.

Ooooh, Shiny: *Shined* Versus *Shone*

Shined and *shone* are two competing past tense forms of the verb *shine*. Some (but not all) sources recommend using *shined* when the verb has an object and *shone* when it does not. An object is something that is the target of the verb's action. A subject is something or someone who takes the action.

Aardvark shined the light in Squiggly's eyes. (*The light* is the object of the verb *shined*. It is the thing being shined by Aardvark, who is the subject.)

The light shone brightly. (The verb *shone* has no object in this sentence. In this sentence *the light* is the subject.)

OF MICE AND MEANINGS: THE PREPOSITION *OF*

Of is a preposition, and although it's not an inherently evil word, overusing it can make your writing sound bloated, passive, and fussy.

She is the wife of George. (bad)

She is George's wife. (better)

Jump off of the dock. (bad)

Jump off the dock. (better)

Of course, *of* sometimes comes in handy. For example, you have to write *Bring me <u>a bucket of water</u>* instead of *Bring me a <u>water bucket</u>* to make your meaning clear.

I also find *of* to be useful when I'm dealing with a complex trail of possession. I find it easier to follow something like *He's the cousin of my neighbor's brother* than *He's my neighbor's brother's cousin*.

Finally, although it's wordy and the *of* is unnecessary, the standard accepted idiom is *a couple of* instead of *a couple*. You have a couple of marimbas, a couple of friends, and a couple of feather boas.

Bring me a water bucket.

Bring me a bucket of water.

Will She Ever Complete a Thought? The E-mail Ellipsis

Some people go overboard with ellipses. You know what I mean; they use ellipses instead of any other form of punctuation. For some reason, it's more common in e-mail than on paper. But these ellipsis abusers aren't all wrong. One use of ellipses is to indicate a pause or a break in the writer's train of thought. It can show that time has passed, a list is unfinished, or a speaker has trailed off in the middle of a sentence or left something unsaid. Nevertheless, most people who use ellipses in e-mail overdo it—a lot. If you recognize yourself in this tip, consider using a period or dash from time to time.

There's a Name for That? Neologisms

Neologism is just a fancy name for a new word that's in the way station between common use and making it into a dictionary. If you want to impress (or annoy) your friends, make up a bunch of words and call yourself a neologist.

A good neologism will capture the essence of a new idea and express it in a way that's familiar enough to make people say, "Ah, yes," when they hear it. Neologisms sometimes use familiar parts of existing words. For example, Watergate is the source for a multitude of -gate scandals, you'd likely recognize that a nicotini is a nicotine-laced martini, and a locavore is a carnivore, herbivore, or omnivore gone local.

Bart Versus Bard, the Linguistic Genius: The Simpsons

Believe it or not, *The Simpsons* (yes, the long-running Fox network cartoon) is a favorite of linguists for its wordplay, and some have compared it to Shakespeare for the sheer number of new words and phrases it has introduced into English. You may even call the characters neologists. Examples include *meh* (indicates lack of excitement or interest in something), *d'oh* (an exclamation you make after doing something stupid), *cromulent* (meaning that something, especially a word, is well formed or acceptable), and *cheese-eating-surrender-monkeys* (an insult to the French). A cartoon it may be, but there must be some pretty language-savvy writers behind the scenes with a knack for neologisms.

You've Got a Grammar Problem? *Have Got*

When AOL belts out *You've got mail,* should your language sensibilities be offended? Some people grouse that "have got" is incorrect or redundant, but grammar experts disagree. *Have got* is informal and can be used to add emphasis. If you've caught someone in a crime, it's stronger to shout, "I've got you now!" than "I have you now." *Have got* is also more forceful than *must. I have got to go* is stronger than *I must go.* Still, even though *have got* is perfectly allowable, it drives some people bonkers, so it's probably better to avoid it in formal writing.

QUIZ: THROUGH THE LOOKING GLASS: *THREW* VERSUS *THRU* VERSUS *THROUGH*

Which is incorrect?

> **a. Aardvark threw the ball at the peeves.**
> **b. It went right thru them.**
> **c. He decided he was through with games.**

The answer and an explanation are on page 223.

EARL GREY TEA: *GRAY* VERSUS *GREY*

Grey is the preferred British spelling, whereas *gray* is more popular in America. You can remember the difference by thinking that the *a* in *gray* is for *American*. If that's too U.S.-centric for you, think of the *e* in *grey* as standing for *England*, but then you'll tick off the people in Australia, Ireland, Wales, and Canada.

I'm American, but I enjoy Earl Grey tea (named after Charles Grey, 2nd Earl Grey, the British prime minister from 1830 to 1834) and regularly look at my tea box, so I was often confused about the spelling before I came up with the *a*-is-for-American memory trick.

Begs the Question

"Begs the question" is a specific phrase from formal logic that is often misused in casual conversation. Its proper use is to indicate that someone has made a conclusion based on a premise that lacks support.

For example, let's say Squiggly is trying to convince Aardvark that chocolate is healthful, and he argues that chocolate grows on trees, so it must be healthful. Aardvark could rightly say there's no proof that something is good for you simply because it grows on a tree. Some things that grow on trees are poisonous. So Squiggly's argument is based on a faulty premise.

Aardvark could correctly say that Squiggly's argument begs the question. What does growing on trees have to do with being healthful, anyway?

I remember what *begs the question* means by thinking that the argument raises a specific question—it begs **the** specific question—*What's your support for that premise?* Or, more informally, *What does that have to do with anything?*

Unfortunately, people often mistakenly use *begs the question* to introduce a clever or obvious question. It's often used to mean "raises the question," as in the following incorrect examples.

When officials are caught in scandals, it begs the question, aren't any decent people running for office?

His dog ran away, which begs the question, why wasn't the dog on a leash.

The quick and dirty tip is to remember that when something begs the question, it begs *the specific* question: what is your support for that premise?

HERB CAEN WAY . . . : THE ELLIPSIS IN JOURNALISM

Although it's not widely endorsed, a few famous newspaper writers have successfully used ellipses instead of periods to separate their rambling thoughts. Larry King heartily used ellipses in his long-running, gossipy *USA Today* column, as did Herb Caen in his also long-running, gossipy *San Francisco Chronicle* column, "It's News to Me." In fact, Herb Caen is reported to have coined the phrase "three-dot journalism" to describe such writing, and he was so beloved in San Francisco that when he died the city named a street after him—and included an ellipsis in the name: Herb Caen Way . . . .

WHAT KIND OF GRAMMAR SNOB ARE YOU? *IT IS I* VERSUS *IT IS ME*

When pronouns follow linking verbs, such as *is*, they should be in the subject case. That means when you answer a call, the proper answer is, "It is I," or "This is she," rather than "That's me." But most grammarians agree that to speak in such a manner sounds pedantic and, in reality, most people say "That's me." We wring our hands and try to decide whether to advise you to use the correct form or the common form because either choice will sound wrong to some people. If you love traditional English, say "It is I." If you like to sound like everyone else, say, "It's me."

Don't Initiate a Conversate

Why, why, why do people think they need to make up longer forms of perfectly good words to sound smarter? *Converse* means "to talk." It's already a fancy way of saying something simple:

They rarely conversed.

To turn *converse* into *conversate* is even worse:

They rarely conversated.

Linguists believe *conversate* is a recent back-formation from *conversation*. For example, people who were trying to figure out what word they should use presume that because words like *hibernation*, *obligation*, and *congregation* become *hibernate*, *obligate*, and *congregate*, *conversation* should become *conversate*. But it shouldn't. The right word is *converse*, and the better word is usually *talk*.

Completely Dead: Modifying Absolutes

Can you really be more dead than dead? If you go quietly in your sleep, are you less dead than if you've been chopped into bits? I think not. So *dead* (like **unique**, **perfect**, and **mortal**) is considered an absolute and usually shouldn't be modified with words like "the most" or "extremely." To say someone is "completely dead" or "very dead" is considered bad form, although occasionally it may make sense to modify an absolute for emphasis. If Big Lips Johnny is questioning whether you've completed your hit, go ahead and say, "Yeah, boss, he's totally dead." Grammar police are the least of your concerns.

Word Scramble: Absolutely Ungradable

Another name used to describe absolute words is **ungradable**. It means that you can't "grade" or apply degrees to them. See if you can unscramble the improperly graded adjectives below.

tiequ eadd_____

a letlit nantperg_____

revy rideram_____

rome cerfpet_____

giltshyl blisspimoe_____

celtmoplye reef_____

ryev tomral_____

The answer key is on page 223.

It's Been Ages: Writing About Ages

When writing out ages, notice when the hyphen is used. When the age is an adjective that comes before the noun and modifies the noun, or when the age is a noun, hyphenate.

Five-year-old Nina loves to eat ice cream.

The adorable five-year-old loves ice cream.

Nina is a five-year-old. (*Girl* is implied—a five-year-old girl—so the hyphenated adjective is coming before the implied noun it modifies.)

When the age is part of an adjective phrase after the noun, don't hyphenate.

Nina is five years old.

Santa Does Grammar: Phrase Versus Clause

Words that work together but don't contain a verb are called a phrase.

We sat <u>under the boardwalk</u>. (a prepositional phrase)

Aardvark enjoys <u>fishing at the lake</u>. (a gerund phrase)

<u>The shiny, happy people</u> held hands. (a noun phrase)

Words that work together and contain a subject and verb are called a clause.

I remember that a clause needs a verb by thinking that Santa Claus is an action guy. He makes toys all year, flies through the air on a sleigh, and hits millions of chimneys in one night, so a clause needs an action word—a verb.

If a clause could stand on its own as a sentence, it is called a main clause or an independent clause.

Santa Claus rides a sleigh.

Santa Claus finds another way in when there isn't a chimney.

If a clause couldn't stand on its own as a sentence, it's called a dependent clause or a subordinate clause.

Santa makes good time <u>because he rides a sleigh</u>.

<u>Since Santa Claus finds another way in when there isn't a chimney</u>, he can still visit kids who live in apartments.

Highlighting Words: Italics, Underlining, and Quotation Marks

When you use a word in a sentence but you don't intend the meaning of the word, you need to highlight it in some way so your readers don't get confused. You've already seen such highlighting a lot in this book—we have mainly used italics, but words can also be highlighted with underlining, bolding, or quotation marks.

Advice ends in *ice*.

The *e* in *stationery* stands for *envelope*.

Italics work well on paper but are hard to read online. Underlining doesn't work well online either, since it makes your word look like a link. We use quotation marks on the Grammar Girl website.

Ooooh, Scary! Scare Quotes

I bet you've seen scare quotes or sneer quotes—quotation marks put around a word to show that the writer doesn't buy into the meaning. If I wrote that women achieved "equality" when they were granted the right to vote in 1920, the quotation marks show that I don't believe the right to vote equaled equality. More often, though, scare quotes are used to impart a sense of irony or disdain. They're especially common when people are being nasty.

She's so "stylish" with her unwashed hair, last year's clothes, and mismatched socks.

Don't you just hate the "caring" person who said that?

Borked: Aptronyms and Eponyms

Although it's a bit heavy-handed, you can imbue characters with personality by using aptronyms: names that suit the owner's personality or profession. A fallen priest may be Father Sin or a persnickety woman may be Mrs. Fussbudget. For laughs, publications sometimes print names of real people whose names are strangely suited to their professions.

The opposite of aptronyms are eponyms: words derived from someone's name. For example, in the sitcom *Friends* the phrase *pulling a Monica* was used to describe a screwup. In real life, the word *Borked* has come to mean attacking someone politically after the contentious (and failed) Supreme Court nomination hearings for U.S. judge Robert Bork.

Because It's a Fragment: Starting a Sentence with *Because*

Because is a subordinating conjunction—clauses beginning with *because* are dependent clauses; they need a main clause. Without a main clause, you have a sentence fragment.

Because it snowed. (fragment)

The main clause can come at the beginning or the end of the sentence, however. You just need it in there somewhere.

Because it snowed, <u>we had hot chocolate for lunch</u>.

<u>We had hot chocolate for lunch</u> because it snowed.

In the first example, the main clause comes after the comma and explains the subordinated part. Suddenly, it's not a sentence fragment; it's a complete sentence with a dependent clause followed by a main clause.

QUIZ: COUNSELOR TROI AND THE COUNCIL OF NINE: *COUNSEL* VERSUS *COUNCIL*

Choose the two correct sentences.

> **a.** In *Star Trek: The Next Generation*, Deanna Troi counseled the captain and crew.
>
> **b.** In *Star Trek: The Next Generation*, Deanna Troi counciled the captain and crew.
>
> **c.** In Greek mythology, the gods formed the Counsel of Nine, which created Pandora's box.
>
> **d.** In Greek mythology, the gods formed the Council of Nine, which created Pandora's box.

The answer and an explanation are on page 224.

SOME FRIENDLY ADVICE

This is going to sound weird coming from Grammar Girl, but when you first sit down to write—whether it's nonfiction or creative writing—just write. Don't think about grammar, punctuation, or spelling. If it's nonfiction and you've done your research, you have your facts, and you've figured out the organization ahead of time (or you're feeling your way through), just write. If you're doing creative writing, just write. If you're yelling at yourself for some stupid word choice or agonizing about whether you need a comma, you'll never move on. Don't worry about it; that's what revisions are for.

WORD SEARCH: SPELLING BEE WORDS

Noah Webster's *Blue-backed Speller* was an important inspiration for the first American spelling bees. Today, the official dictionary for the Scripps National Spelling Bee is *Webster's Third New International Dictionary, Unabridged,* and the publisher's website lists these words, among others, as those that are most commonly misspelled.

The answer key is on page 224.

N	V	S	I	D	I	Y	E	B	N	N	T
O	I	V	N	K	A	H	X	I	O	E	P
G	L	L	D	N	T	C	H	X	T	T	I
Z	L	L	E	O	H	O	I	Q	I	I	E
D	A	E	P	W	L	N	L	I	C	L	C
Y	I	P	E	L	E	S	A	B	E	L	E
P	N	S	N	E	T	C	R	X	A	E	R
C	Y	S	D	D	E	I	A	O	B	T	V
V	C	I	E	G	G	E	T	I	L	A	C
H	B	M	N	E	E	N	E	E	E	S	P
B	U	M	C	I	L	T	D	U	N	D	M
O	R	U	E	D	I	I	F	G	K	W	E
B	E	U	V	P	V	O	R	A	Q	S	M
W	A	C	O	F	I	U	M	E	Q	B	S
Q	U	A	Y	Z	R	S	Y	L	M	I	E
D	N	V	Z	S	P	W	E	I	R	D	S
E	C	N	E	R	R	U	C	C	O	D	K

ATHLETE	LEAGUE	SATELLITE
BUREAU	MISSPELL	VACUUM
CONSCIENTIOUS	NOTICEABLE	VILLAIN
EXHILARATE	OCCURRENCE	WEIRD
INDEPENDENCE	PRIVILEGE	
KNOWLEDGE	RECEIPT	

Quiz, Word Scramble, and Word Search Answers

The answer is (d). *Welcome* can be many things: a noun, a verb, an adjective, and an interjection. But *welcomed* is the past tense form of the verb to *welcome*, not an adjective.

WEEK 2 FRIDAY

The unscrambled words, in order, are as follows: personal (e.g., *he*, *she*), possessive (e.g., *my*, *your*), demonstrative (e.g., *these*), indefinite (e.g., *everyone*), relative (e.g., *which*, *that*), and interrogative (e.g., *who*).

There are other classes of pronouns; for example, some people consider reflexive pronouns to be a separate class and other people consider them to be a subset of personal pronouns.

WEEK 3 FRIDAY

All of the sentences are correct. Optical discs like CDs are spelled with a *c*, and other kinds of computer storage media such as floppy drives and external hard drives are spelled with a *k*. Although there is some disagreement, *Stedman's* medical dictionary recommends the spelling *disc* for all medical uses. You can remember that *optical* has a *c* in it and *disc* for optical drives and for biology (like your optic nerve) also are spelled with a *c*.

WEEK 4 FRIDAY

The answer is (b). *Latter* means "last" (note that both start with *l*) and *former* means "first" (note that both start with *f*). Only use these terms when distinguishing between two choices, and use them sparingly because they confuse many people. Even if your readers know the meaning, they have to go back to the previous sentence to find the answer. Avoid the words in speech because listeners can't go back and review what you said in the previous sentence (and if they try, they'll probably miss what you say next).

WEEK 5 FRIDAY

The answer is (a). Although either spelling is acceptable, it's more common to see the one-word spelling—*cannot*. A quick and dirty memory tip is to think of a magician taunting a rabbit with a carrot saying, "You cannot have the carrot." Extend the *r*'s in *carrot* to the bottom of the line and, voilà, the word *carrot* turns into *cannot*.

WEEK 6 FRIDAY

The unscrambled words, in order, are as follows: awoke (past of *awake*), became (past of *become*), sought (past of *seek*), mistook (past of *mistake*), and froze (past of *freeze*).

WEEK 7 FRIDAY

The correct spelling in America is *canceled*, choice (b). In Britain, it is spelled with two *l*'s: *cancelled*. Blame Noah Webster! (For more on Noah Webster, see page 16, Wednesday.)

WEEK 8 FRIDAY

The answer is (a). In most cases, *different from* is preferred over *different than*. The quick and dirty tip is that *different* has two *f*'s in the middle, so you choose the preposition that starts with *f* (*from*).

R	L	E	B	E	W	S	M	R	Z	Z	P
U	Z	A	A	R	E	F	A	C	E	F	T
K	W	D	E	L	C	I	H	L	Z	I	R
R	K	S	S	F	L	L	M	X	S	G	E
A	K	C	M	D	Y	I	U	I	T	A	K
V	N	H	O	T	E	B	R	G	U	L	H
D	E	A	R	U	N	U	V	R	H	Y	A
R	T	D	G	P	T	N	A	K	E	P	K
A	R	E	A	A	U	G	O	N	V	U	I
A	A	N	S	K	H	A	S	O	J	N	G
U	G	F	B	C	L	P	M	X	D	A
G	R	R	O	S	C	O	X	U	F	I	I
R	E	E	R	F	Y	W	X	M	L	T	V
A	D	U	D	F	R	H	G	M	A	D	C
T	N	D	N	W	E	W	N	W	Z	V	W
I	I	E	P	F	I	D	A	H	I	J	D
N	K	S	A	G	J	U	U	L	P	Q	L

WEEK 9 **FRIDAY**

The correct answer is (b). *Dragged* is the proper past tense form of *drag*. *Drug* is used as the past tense in dialects most commonly found in the southern United States. Just say no to *drug*!

WEEK 10 **FRIDAY**

The unscrambled words, in order, are as follows: because, despite, though, unless, and whenever.

WEEK 11 **FRIDAY**

The order, from worst to best, is (a), (b), (c). *The reason is because* [in choice (a)] is a redundant phrase. (B) is better, but unnecessarily wordy. (C) avoids redundancies and gets the point across in fewer words.

WEEK 12 **FRIDAY**

Although you often hear people use *quote* as a noun, technically, it's only a verb, so (a) is incorrect. Proper use: *I want to quote you. Is this the correct quotation?*

```
Y  V  L  T  E  E  R  C  S  I  D  L  H
U  H  O  D  E  R  I  E  R  B  R  T  G
W  I  A  I  R  W  E  O  L  U  A  T  S
D  G  U  F  A  I  R  H  N  N  O  G  P
I  R  Z  X  B  L  B  U  T  A  B  Y  C
S  E  I  H  X  M  J  P  K  R  X  Y  K
C  R  C  E  Z  I  B  Z  R  A  E  H  S
R  Z  A  Z  H  S  K  F  F  F  N  Y  U
E  N  M  E  E  T  E  R  J  F  X  Q  S
T  E  H  N  H  S  M  Y  E  B  E  A  R
E  G  Z  P  S  U  B  O  U  E  K  F  R
N  X  B  U  A  R  O  U  O  H  H  T  O
A  M  O  J  Z  B  E  R  M  S  K  S  S
O  M  R  E  J  N  Q  E  N  Z  E  E  S
L  R  E  L  O  Q  Z  T  S  Q  P  N  H
E  T  D  L  S  H  E  R  E  F  A  R  E
U  X  Y  Z  X  U  S  Z  H  R  P  Y  V
```

(B) and (d) are incorrect. Collections either *comprise* a list of their parts or are *composed of* a list of their parts.

The unscrambled words, in order, are as follows: actually (as in *Write what you _actually_ mean*), little (as in *Your writing will be a _little_ better*), pretty (as in *She _pretty much_ avoided the issue*), really (as in *Write what you _really_ mean*), rather (as in *He's a _rather_ happy bloke*).

Dos and don'ts, answer (b), is correct. Although it looks strange because of the apostrophe in *don't,* there's no special rule for making contractions plural. Simply add an *s* to the end as you would any other word.

The correct sentence is (b). *And* is a conjunction and *to* is a preposition; they don't serve the same functions in a sentence. In this case, *to* is part of the infinitive verb phrase *to download.*

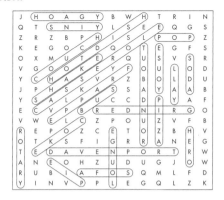

WEEK 17 **FRIDAY**

Trick question! They're all correct. *Sort, kind,* and *type* mean the same thing and can be used interchangeably.

WEEK 18 **FRIDAY**

The unscrambled words, in order, are as follows: noun, pronoun, verb, adjective, adverb, preposition, conjunction, and interjection.

Not everyone agrees on this list. Some people would eliminate interjections, add articles or determiners, or split verbs into lexical verbs and auxiliary verbs.

WEEK 19 **FRIDAY**

The correct sentence is (a). *Loose* means not tight; *lose* means to misplace. A quick and dirty tip is to remember that *loose* has two *o*'s by remembering the phrase *loose as a goose*, where *goose* also has two *o*'s. (*Loose as a goose* is an idiom that means "relaxed.")

WEEK 20 **FRIDAY**

The correct sentence is (b). You don't want to founder or flounder in college, but *flounder* means to be confused and thrash around clumsily, and *founder* means to fail completely. A flounder is also a kind of fish, so you can remember that fish thrash around clumsily when out of their element.

```
Y  H  L  A  V  E  A  I  D  E  M  G  U  P  D
A  I  M  E  A  N  A  J  T  D  J  X  K  I  A
E  K  W  Y  G  O  L  O  E  H  C  R  A  Q  I
P  E  W  Y  J  I  M  L  E  V  L  F  W  G  D
A  N  K  O  T  W  K  Z  S  D  Y  T  O  Y  E
E  C  M  A  N  E  U  V  E  R  R  K  V  S  A
D  Y  E  S  T  R  O  G  E  N  L  I  B  X  P
I  C  Z  B  G  M  A  N  O  E  U  V  R  E  O
A  L  V  S  U  T  E  O  F  J  G  J  W  Y  L
T  O  C  I  D  E  P  O  H  T  R  O  O  J  C
R  P  D  Y  A  R  C  H  A  E  O  L  O  G  Y
I  E  T  E  S  R  Q  F  E  T  U  S  A  Y  C
C  D  D  B  C  I  R  T  A  I  D  E  P  M  N
J  I  U  O  E  S  T  R  O  G  E  N  J  Q  E
N  A  V  O  R  T  H  O  P  A  E  D  I  C  P
V  G  Y  B  H  T  L  A  V  E  I  D  E  M  X
J  O  A  X  F  U  V  A  I  M  E  K  U  E  L
Z  U  O  E  Q  U  J  L  Q  D  H  H  C  N  W
Z  Z  T  H  P  Q  I  D  N  Y  Q  J  K  L  T
A  N  E  M  I  A  I  M  E  A  K  U  E  L  E
```

WEEK 21 **FRIDAY**

The answer is (a). *Pique*, from a French word for *prick*, means to excite. You want to excite people's interest. I know peeking can be exciting, and *peak* sounds like the top you want to reach, but you don't peek or peak anyone's interest.

WEEK 22 **FRIDAY**

The unscrambled words, in order, are as follows: advice, bravery, courage, education, freedom, honor, loyalty, pain, and trust.

WEEK 23 **FRIDAY**

Trick question! Both are correct. The short answer is that *advisor* and *adviser* are interchangeable. The long answer is that a few sources prefer *adviser* with an *e*, so it's probably better to use that form; but don't let anyone tell you *advisor* is wrong.

WEEK 24 **TUESDAY**

The answer is (b). I hope you said (b)! The correct word is *anyway*. *Anyways* is considered a nonstandard form of the word *anyway* and is incorrect.

WEEK 24 **FRIDAY**

The answer is (a). The most accepted spelling of the word is *barbecue* because it most closely resembles the word from which it's derived—*barbacoa*. The shorter forms, such as *bar-b-q*, are just abbreviations that play on the sounds from the syllables *be* (*b*) and *cue* (*q*). Most sources say the Spanish adopted the word *barbacoa* from local populations they encountered in the Caribbean who used the word to describe the wooden frameworks they used to cook meat.

WEEK 24 SUNDAY

```
M  G  Q  K  V  F  R  A  M  E  D  L  X
R  E  C  S  P  I  L  L  E  D  I  V  Y
D  H  L  E  A  R  N  E  D  N  Y  I  C
A  E  W  K  H  J  L  R  T  L  I  P  S
D  G  L  U  S  X  E  Q  L  D  U  N  N
N  E  B  I  T  L  I  O  P  S  H  X  D
J  Q  L  J  O  B  U  R  N  E  D  R  O
S  F  P  L  Z  P  N  Y  C  W  E  G  N
T  W  O  G  E  D  S  P  Y  A  Q  M  R
S  A  D  E  Y  P  H  J  M  H  Q  E  P
H  Z  F  R  X  S  E  D  O  W  C  K
J  O  R  B  E  E  D  O  R  K  P  D  E
P  T  S  Y  U  A  T  E  Q  C  T  K  L
G  T  P  N  J  R  M  X  P  V  P  G  U
D  Z  E  E  Q  N  N  T  O  A  A  S  D
J  C  L  F  L  T  O  T  N  P  E  B  Q
E  H  T  M  J  R  R  Q  E  M  L  L  F
```

WEEK 25 FRIDAY

(B) is incorrect. *Alot* is not a word. *A lot* means "a large number" or "very much." *Allot* means "to parcel out."

WEEK 26 FRIDAY

The unscrambled words, in order, are as follows: could, might, must, need, shall, and would.

WEEK 27 FRIDAY

It's a close call but, if I had to choose, I'd say (a) is best. *In spite of* and *despite* mean the same thing and are interchangeable, but some people prefer *despite* because it is shorter. *In despite of* is just plain wrong.

WEEK 27 SUNDAY

The hint was *tents* and *porpoises* to help you remember that the correct answer (b) is two things: intents and purposes.

G	H	H	Q	G	X	G	A	D	N	E	G	A			
P	X	S	C	S	A	P	P	E	N	D	I	X			
W	O	M	T	U	W	R	T	G	K	S	S	U			
Z	R	E	Q	P	C	A	R	A	D	I	U	S			
S	E	M	E	M	A	I	D	E	M	X	T	N			
R	A	O	W	A	X	W	Z	W	N	A	A	L			
W	K	R	L	C	R	N	N	B	G	V	I	L			
N	T	A	I	N	M	U	L	A	X	B	H	L			
I	G	N	A	L	U	M	R	O	F	E	G	O			
N	V	D	E	T	M	O	L	N	V	A	U	C			
D	L	U	V	L	U	Q	H	A	I	C	E	U			
E	L	M	Q	G	O	M	O	Q	R	M	O	S			
X	V	C	O	A	U	V	A	D	U	V	C	U			
F	Q	A	T	A	D	R	E	I	S	O	A	W			
O	R	O	J	Z	G	B	Q	L	Z	W	B	X			
C	I	P	T	B	I	F	Y	R	Q	M	W	G			

WEEK 29 **FRIDAY**

Both (a) and (d) are correct. *Currant* (with an *a*) is the fruit. A quick and dirty tip is that *currant* ends with the word *ant*, and ants eat fruit.

WEEK 30 **FRIDAY**

The unscrambled phrases, in order, are as follows: big fish in a small pond, curiosity killed the cat, dead as a doornail, have a nice day, like the plague, peas in a pod, slept like a log, stubborn as a mule, *and* sold like hotcakes.

WEEK 31 **FRIDAY**

The answer is (b). Although people often believe *verbal* means spoken, it actually refers to both written and spoken words. For example, parts of the written SAT measure your verbal skills. *Oral* is the proper adjective to indicate that words are spoken.

WEEK 32 **FRIDAY**

The correct wording is (a), to "home in" on something. Think of a homing pigeon homing in on its destination. (To hone something means to sharpen it.)

W	J	O	Q	C	A	I	R	E	T	I	R	C
V	Y	S	Q	K	I	N	E	T	I	C	T	A
K	A	P	B	J	J	M	P	F	L	A	S	U
A	J	M	A	A	T	Y	A	A	C	C	I	N
L	J	W	F	M	F	H	T	X	A	T	N	X
E	R	A	F	U	R	P	H	A	T	U	O	U
I	Z	I	J	A	E	A	O	I	A	S	G	X
D	O	G	V	R	W	R	S	O	S	J	A	X
O	C	L	J	T	F	G	E	N	T	G	T	N
S	T	A	D	V	A	I	K	A	R	K	O	G
C	O	T	Q	I	F	L	C	R	O	U	R	V
O	P	S	A	D	R	L	T	A	P	D	P	C
P	U	O	X	U	C	A	O	P	H	O	O	N
E	S	N	K	S	A	C	S	Y	E	S	R	M
G	J	Q	B	Y	S	A	T	S	C	E	T	A
L	G	P	G	Y	P	O	R	T	N	E	S	L
D	V	A	H	L	K	Y	Q	L	P	D	Z	R

WEEK 33 **FRIDAY**

The answer is (a). Conservative language folks believe that *nauseous* should be used only to mean "to induce nausea." To say you are nauseous is to say something bad about yourself!

WEEK 34 **FRIDAY**

The unscrambled phrases, in order, are as follows: go ahead and, brief moment, end result, join together, equal halves, true fact, *and* point in time.

WEEK 35 **FRIDAY**

The correct sentence is (a). *Assure* is the only one of the three words that means "to reassure someone or to promise." *Ensure* chiefly means "to make certain or to guarantee." Although in some cases *insure* can be interchangeable with *ensure*, it is easiest to keep these words straight by reserving *insure* for references to insurance.

WEEK 36 **FRIDAY**

Only (a) is correct in formal writing. The tilde is acceptable as shorthand to show an approximation, as in (b) but in formal writing you should write out the words. The tilde can be used to show a range of numbers in some languages, but not in English.

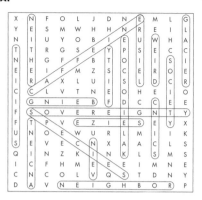

Answer (b) is incorrect because the names of specific historical periods are capitalized. Therefore, *Great Depression* is capitalized even though *great* and *depression* are not capitalized when they are used as common nouns.

WEEK 38 FRIDAY

The unscrambled words, in order, are as follows: anyway, certainly, finally, hence, instead, likewise, namely, and therefore.

WEEK 38 SUNDAY

Yes! *Everyone* and *everybody* mean the same thing and are interchangeable.

WEEK 39 FRIDAY

(B) and (d) are incorrect. When making a compound word plural, you make the noun part plural. They are your sisters, and *in-law* just describes what kind of sisters they are; and they are attorneys and *general* just describes what kind of attorneys they are.

WEEK 40 FRIDAY

The correct sentence is (a). A crevasse is a large, deep gap. A crevice is a smaller fissure, for example, a crack you'd find in a sidewalk.

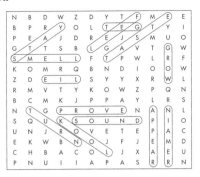

(B) and (d) are incorrect. You wreak (not wreck) havoc, and the proper past tense form of *wreak* is **wreaked**. *Wrought* is the archaic past tense form of *work* and is usually seen only as an adjective or in poems today.

The unscrambled words, in order, are as follows: aircraft, deer, moose, salmon, and sheep.

Every option is correct. The rule for *nor* is the same as the rule for *or*, and the rule applies whether the subjects are proper nouns or pronouns. Some style books recommend always putting the plural subject last and using a plural verb when you have a singular and plural subject, except when the subject is *I*. If you were following this rule, then (c) would be incorrect.

The answer is (b). Although *and/or*, (a), is an acceptable way to show that one or both things are options in informal writing (*please bring chips and/or cookies to the party*), it's almost always a bad choice in formal writing. You can usually make your meaning clearer by spelling out what you mean. Choice (c) was a close second because the drug does both treat and prevent the flu, but (b) is best because it more clearly explains how the drug would be used by one individual.

WEEK 44 SUNDAY

E	P	N	W	(E)	(E)	B	(E)	(E)	L	K	H
E	V	V	Y	L	T	F	X	L	(N)	B	Z
M	Y	Q	L	B	A	G	O	B	O	Y	M
E	U	J	F	I	G	U	L	I	I	(E)	L
F	I	(C)	(E)	S	I	L	E	S	T	M	J
L	(S)	U	D	S	T	G	T	S	A	A	(A)
D	U	B	E	O	A	(S)	(E)	O	I	C	N
(T)	O	I	P	P	(F)	U	(D)	P	D	E	A
E	R	C	X	N	J	P	I	M	A	R	C
M	B	U	(E)	(U)	(T)	P	G	O	L	A	E
U	E	L	X	P	N	E	N	C	G	T	P
L	C	A	G	J	E	D	O	N	I	(E)	H
E	E	R	Y	U	G	I	T	(I)	(D)	O	A
N	L	(Y)	A	Y	N	T	I	A	A	K	L
(T)	L	W	U	L	(I)	A	O	I	X	M	I
T	(I)	M	N	W	S	T	(N)	Y	N	P	Z
T	P	E	(T	I	M	E)	(D)	T	Z	W	(E)

WEEK 45 FRIDAY

The answer is (b). *Sic* is Latin for "thus," "so," "as such," or "in such manner," but the various misinterpretations—such as *spelling incorrect*—can help you remember what it's used for. "Bob went their [*sic*] for dinner.

WEEK 46 THURSDAY

The answer is (c). If you come upon a case where you have two related numbers in the same sentence, you should write them both as numerals if you would write one as a numeral. The idea is to write them the same way when they are in the same sentence. So even though you would normally write out the word *two,* in this case you use the numeral (2) so it matches the 12.

WEEK 46 FRIDAY

The answer is (c). To avoid confusion by having two numerals next to each other, you should write the words for the smaller of the two numbers.

WEEK 47 FRIDAY

The answer is (b). A round number in the millions or higher is typically written as a combination of the numeral with the word *million, billion,* etc. The only choice that is technically incorrect is

(d) (if you are trying to write 35 million). As it is written, (d) is a million more than 35 million.

The unscrambled words, in order, are as follows: Angelino (Los Angeles), Austinite (Austin), Bostonian (Boston), Houstonian (Houston), Minneapolitan (Minneapolis), and Phoenician (Phoenix).

WEEK 48 SUNDAY

```
B  K  Z  T  T  V  X  X  F  N  O  I  M
Y  M  J  A  Z  Z  A  G  E  Z  A  S  E
F  V  K  K  Z  E  D  O  W  N  T  G  D
F  W  L  C  A  Z  O  R  P  M  R  B  I
K  A  E  B  E  X  M  L  L  T  A  G  C
S  N  E  U  G  A  H  E  H  T  C  N  A
E  I  N  G  X  X  G  B  P  R  A  X  R
G  S  E  R  Z  C  M  M  O  A  N  C  E
A  U  X  M  W  P  A  Q  F  W  G  A  V
E  P  L  N  O  E  F  M  E  L  A  P  H
L  E  S  S  Y  D  O  C  A  I  M  B  Y
D  R  Y  K  R  X  E  L  S  V  A  O  A
D  B  Y  A  X  U  Q  E  T  I  D  Q  P
I  O  D  E  Z  N  P  Y  E  C  P  G  Z
M  W  T  C  A  T  O  I  R  T  A  P  W
I  L  R  E  W  O  T  S  R  A  E  S  C
C  G  H  C  P  E  X  J  P  N  L  Z  S
```

WEEK 49 FRIDAY

The answer is (c). The correct phrase is *old-fashioned,* with a hyphen. (And, of course, *sundae* is an ice cream dessert, and *Sunday* is a day of the week. Interestingly, *ice cream* comes from an older term, *iced cream*, so maybe someday *old-fashioned* will evolve into *old-fashion.*)

WEEK 50 FRIDAY

Choice (b), *It went right thru them*, is incorrect. Although *thru* has been proposed as a simplified spelling for *through*, it hasn't gained acceptance in standard English. It does make regular appearances in informal contexts such as signs and advertisements.

WEEK 51 FRIDAY

The unscrambled phrases, in order, are as follows: quite dead, a little pregnant, very married, more perfect, slightly impossible, completely free, *and* very mortal.

Just because you can't grade these adjectives doesn't mean you can't add words for emphasis in informal situations, but use caution. Make sure that when you say something is "completely free," it's for emphasis, and when you say "slightly impossible," it's for irony, and not just because you're being careless or redundant.

(A) and (d) are correct. *Counsel* is a verb that means "to give advice" (or a noun describing the advice received as a result of counseling), and *council* is a noun that describes a group of decision makers.

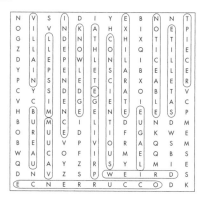

Acknowledgments

Writing a book is a solitary practice, but publishing a book is not. It's shocking how many people are needed to shepherd a book from idea to reality.

Thank you to Richard Rhorer, whose title as director of business development for the Quick and Dirty Tips enterprise doesn't do justice to his role in making this book a reality or in sustaining my daily enthusiasm for my work.

Thank you to the "people in charge," including Brian Napack for ongoing enthusiasm, Dan Farley and Mary Beth Roche for giving the project a green light, and John Sterling, whose earlier contributions are not forgotten.

Thank you to my editor at Henry Holt and Company, Helen Atsma, whose insights, recommendations, vetos, and encouragement made this book significantly better; and to her assistant, Supurna Banerjee. I would also like to thank Sally Doherty, my editor at Holt Books for Young Readers, and all the other people at Holt who made contributions to the success of this book, including copy editors, typesetters, cover designers, marketing people, and salespeople.

Thank you to the illustrator, Arnie Ten, who brought Squiggly,

Aardvark, and the peeves to life as I imagined them and in a way that makes me love them even more.

As is customary to say, but is also true, I am grateful to all these people, but any errors that remain in this book should not fall on their shoulders; they are mine alone.

Thank you to Bonnie Trenga, a frequent guest writer for the Grammar Girl podcast; and Sal Glynn and Charles Carson, occasional guest writers.

Thank you also to the many people who write each week to tell me how the Grammar Girl podcast, e-mail newsletter, or previous book has touched your lives. It is those glimpses that drive me to keep going, to produce more work, and to find new ways to help you learn. I'm not furthering the cause of world peace or curing cancer, but you've made me believe that, in a small way, I do make a difference.

Thank you to Reno's West Street Market, where I wrote much of this book.

The final thank-you goes to my husband, Patrick, who didn't want me to write this book and insisted that I occasionally step away from the computer. As frustrating as that was at times, I grudgingly welcome his tempering influence because I fear that if he were as enthusiastic about my work as I am, it would consume me entirely. When I think about it, I'm glad that he wants more of me rather than being happy to settle for less.

Index

Sarah Shatz

ABOUT THE AUTHOR

Mignon Fogarty is the creator of *Grammar Girl* and the founder and managing director of *Quick and Dirty Tips*. Formerly a magazine writer, technical writer, and entrepreneur, she has a B.A. in English from the University of Washington in Seattle and an M.S. in biology from Stanford University. She lives in Reno, Nevada. Visit her website at www.quickanddirtytips.com and sign up for the free e-mail grammar tips and podcast.